Laplanche

an introduction

Laplanche

an introduction

by Dominique Scarfone

Translated by Dorothée Bonnigal-Katz

New York:
The Unconscious in Translation

Jean Laplanche originally published as *Jean Laplanche* (Paris: Presses Universitaires de France, 1997) ; Primal Fantasy, Fantasies of Origins, Origins of Fantasy originally published as *Fantasme originaire, fantasmes des origines, origines du fantasme* in *Les Temps Modernes*, #215, Volume 19, April 1964. Republished in the series *Textes du XXe siècle* with a new introduction by the authors (Paris: Hachette, 1985); Preface to Beyond the Pleasure Principle origninally published as *Préface* in *Au-delà du principle de Plaisir* (Paris: Presses Universitaires de France, 2010)

Original French version
ISBN 2130484050
© Press Universitaires de France, 1997
108, boulevard Saint-Germain, 75006 Paris

ISBN 978-1-942254-02-7
Library of Congress Control Number: 2014957808

CONTENTS

Preface

Laplanche's immense contribution to psychoanalysis has three main components which can be subsumed under one heading: a critical approach to Freudian thinking. By "critical approach" I mean the capacity to assess the epistemological status of psychoanalytic theory including, among other things, its heuristic power, its internal structure and consistency, and its validity—that is its correspondence to the facts.

The first contribution is his method of reading Freud, his endeavor to submit Freud's own writings to the Freudian method and thereby to distinguish the strong and weak parts of Freud's theorizing with the aim of giving it a clearer and more solid grounding. The second major contribution is his development of a model of key mental processes centered on the concept of translation, a model that extends our understanding of mechanisms that structure the psyche (a model which he can be said to have implemented in 30 years of practical work leading the team that retranslated Freud's complete works into French.) The third contribution is the General Theory of Seduction (GTS) that came as the result of combination of his method of reading Freud and the model of translation. In Laplanche's view the GTS provides psychoanalysis with new foundations. The GTS is not simply one more theory in psychoanalysis nor is it meant to create a "new psychoanalysis." Laplanche introduced the GTS in 1987, in a book he dubbed *New Foundations for Psychoanalysis*; what is new is clearly the foundations, not psychoanalysis itself. The psychoanalysis Laplanche addresses does not call for the epithet "new" because, although the GTS sheds light on clinical practice, it does not call for a new technique, even though it may produce new insights about what goes on in the analytic setting. Practical consequences are left for the practitioner to decide. Laplanche's writings display his trust that his readers can make use of clear and sound concepts to find their own way in their clinical work. Nevertheless, practical tasks are in no way secondary in Laplanche's approach. Indeed, while he may seem to emphasize "pure theory," Laplanche starts from the practical task—the analytic session following the Freudian method—and links this task to re-reading Freudian metapsychology so as to bring it away from Freud's meta-biological and cosmological speculations back within the borders of the anthropological realm.

Just as he did not advocate a "new psychoanalysis," Laplanche never tried to create his own "school." An important aspect of Laplanche's legacy is his freedom to think by himself—he dared criticize not only Freud but also the major exponent of the French post-Freudian movement, his own analyst, Jacques Lacan—and he invites his readers to do the same with the help of the instruments he created: the method of reading Freud and the translational model. For anyone who makes use of such tools, the third element in Laplanche's legacy (the GTS) will easily follow, not merely as one more theory, nor because Laplanche "says so," but as a logical consequence.

Laplanche's critical reading reveals that Freud's abandonment of the seduction theory in 1897 was of cataclysmic importance and its consequences are still with us, notably in the theoretical Babel of contemporary psychoanalysis. As for Laplanche's renewal of the seduction theory, it is both a positive contribution to psychoanalysis and an opportunity for re-structuring Freudian theory, that is to say for re-reading Freud, with new eyes and, in the process, verifying two of Italo Calvino's famous definitions of 'a classic':

- Every rereading of a classic is as much a voyage of discovery as the first reading.
- Every reading of a classic is in fact a rereading.[1]

For Calvino, a classic is a text that, when read for the first time, yields a sense of familiarity, as if we already knew what it was about. But a classic is also a text that, when we re-read it, gives us the feel-

---

1 Calvino, "Why Read the Classics?", *The New York Review of Books*, October 9, 1986.

ing we are reading it for the first time. This is precisely what happens when reading Freud along with Laplanche.

Obviously, one needs not choose among the three main contributions of Laplanche's *œuvre* but, if forced to do so, I would certainly opt for his reading of Freud, for it is there that Laplanche's method was simultaneously developed and demonstrated in practice; the translational model of the mind and the General Theory of Seduction emerged from that reading. Models and theories are perfectible and potentially refutable, but a good method is the necessary tool not only for their construction but also for their revision. Laplanche was very clear about this, he always asked of those collaborating with him to put his own thinking "back to work."

*

My text is intended as an introduction to Laplanche's *œuvre*, a general overview of his work. Part of the series *"Psychanalystes d'aujourd'hui"* established by the Presses Universitaires de France, *"Jean Laplanche"* first appeared in 1997 and therefore doesn't include references to Laplanche's later works. However, the recent publication in English of Laplanche's "Freud and the *Sexual*" is well suited for filling this gap.

The two other pieces in this volume are good illustrations of Laplanche's method of reading Freud, unearthing concepts that Freud himself had not explicitly formulated.

The historical text on primal fantasies by Laplanche and Pontalis which is reprinted here is of paramount importance for anyone wishing to reflect on the nature and function of fantasy in the life of the psyche. It must be stressed, however, that while this work is illustrative of the critical reading of Freud, it does not represent Laplanche's view of the matter. This is often overlooked in the psychoanalytic literature: an author can identify concepts in Freud which he does not necessarily share. Laplanche, for instance, has always been very critical of Freud's contention that fantasies can be inherited genetically. A similar position concerns the concept of *Anlehnung* (literally "leaning-on" but translated by Strachey as *anaclisis*) which was first highlighted by Laplanche and Pontalis in their widely acclaimed *Language of Psychoanalysis*, but which Laplanche went on to reject in favor of the concept of seduction, as I have documented in the first part of the present book.

The short "Preface to *Beyond the Pleasure Principle*" is a very late text by Laplanche. His usual critical gaze is recognizable, notably when remarking on Freud's tautological reasoning about the new theory of the drives and when discussing the concept of "speculation."

Dominique Scarfone

Editorial note

Decisions about translating Laplanche's writing into English have largely been left to each translator. The translations however have been reviewed for terminological consistency and to some degree for some consistency of style. We have taken account of the fact that some of Laplanche's published texts are transcriptions of lectures and that the copy editing of the published texts is less than perfect.

With Laplanche's encouragement, UIT decided to publish the English translations of his work in more or less reverse chronological order. *Sexual: La sexualité élargie au sens freudien*, containing his major work from 2000 to 2006, was the last volume to be published in his lifetime and the first to be published by UIT. Laplanche was eager to be involved in the translation of his work, generous with his time, and gracious in his assistance. The English translation—"Freud and the Sexual"—benefited directly from his guidance. With one important exception, the decisions made for that volume have been carried forward to rest of the UIT series. The note below addresses some issues we faced and offers brief explanations of the decisions made.

Jonathan House
General Editor

Âme/animique – soul/psychic/mental

Laplanche argued that the German *Seele* has the same religious philosophical resonances as does the French *âme* and so *âme* and *animique* should be used for *Seele* and *seelisch* etc. We think the situation is different for 'soul' not only because its use in the sense of 'mind' or 'psyche' is less common in English than is the case for *âme* and *Seele* in French and German, but because adjectival forms 'soulical' and 'soulish', while they exist, are so rare that their use in these texts would be distracting, if not confusing. So, except in rare instances, such as

xi

'apparatus of the soul', we have used 'mind' or 'psyche' and their derivatives.

Après-coup – après-coup

Freud's used the word *Nachträglichkeit* which is an unusual substantive form of the everyday German adjective *nachträglich* (afterwards). Laplanche suggested that the neologism 'afterwardsness' be used as the English translation of the term. We have decided otherwise. Laplanche said more than once that Lacan had the merit of being the first to recognize the conceptual importance of the notion. It was, however, Laplanche and Pontalis in "The Language of Psycho-analysis" who first theorized the concept and it was Laplanche who later developed the theorization more fully. If concepts have nationality, après-coup is French. In the years since Laplanche first advocated 'afterwardsness', the word après-coup has become common in Anglophone psychoanalytic discourse. For that reason, starting with the present volume, we have decided to use après-coup as the English term for the concept.

Étayage – leaning-on

Étayage is the French translation of the German word *Anlehnung* which Strachey, in the Standard Edition, renders as 'anaclisis' – a cognate of the Greek *anaklinein* (ἀνακλίνω - leaning on). In translating Laplanche's work there is a long standing debate about the relative merits of translating *étayage* by 'leaning-on' or by 'propping'. In Jeffrey Mehlman's translation of Life and Death, he used 'propping' often in the reflexive form. Laplanche preferred 'leaning-on' to emphasize the activity of the drive leaning-on the instinct, an activity which tends to be obscured. For this series, we have chosen to use 'leaning-on'.

Étrangèreté – **strangerness**

Étrangèreté is a neologism combining the meanings of *étrange*, 'strange', and *étranger*, 'foreigner'. We render it with the neologism "strangerness" which we hope conveys the same meaning and evokes the more or less the same associations.

Théorie de la séduction généralisée – **General Theory of Seduction**

Some translators have rendered the phrase 'theory of generalized seduction' which is a reasonable choice but loses Laplanche's intended echo of the distinction between Einstein's general and special theories of relativity. The special theory of seduction is Freud's theory of seduction, and it is 'special' or 'specific' in the sense that it explains the origins of specific psychopathologic entities: hysteria and other neuroses of defense. The General Theory of Seduction is concerned with the origin of the human subject.

Jean Laplanche

by Dominique Scarfone

Translated by Dorothée Bonnigal-Katz

The Psychoanalyst and the Stars

To anyone closely acquainted with the development of Jean Laplanche's ideas, the title of his collection of articles, *The Unfinished Copernican Revolution*,[1] seems most appropriate. As is commonly known, the reference to Copernicus comes from Freud, who located himself, along with Darwin, in the lineage of the famous astronomer. Laplanche did not spend his nights peering obsessively through a telescope. Yet the astronomical metaphor runs through his work in more than one way. In 1980, for instance, in an interview with the French daily *Le Monde*, Laplanche drew a parallel between psychoanalysis and astronomy: "It is wrong to assume that any knowledge, however deep it might be, results in some material increase in our power: what is the power wielded by astronomy, the most ancient of all sciences? On the stars, it exerts none. As for the astronaut, he might rely on universal gravitation to thread his way between the stars but certainly not to change their course. To Freud, the unconscious is like the stars, and it is even more unalterable than they are because it is not subject to time. So let me tell you how amazed I am to see how psychoanalyzed man sometimes manages to thread his way between Freud's

---

1 Translator's note: The author is referring to *La révolution copernicienne inachevée*, a collection that includes the essay "The Unfinished Copernican Revolution." Some of the essays published in *La révolution copernicienne inachevée* (including "The Unfinished Copernican Revolution") have been translated into English and can be found in *Essays on Otherness*.

stars. . . ."[2] This improvised metaphor seems especially well suited to its author, who may be regarded as an astronomer of Freudian psychoanalysis—an astronomer rather than a Freudologist, an historian or archeologist of Freudianism. An astronomer or an astronaut of psychoanalysis, Laplanche does not strive to shift the celestial bodies discovered by Freud: as he points out in the passage just quoted, the unconscious is more unalterable than even the stars. Laplanche ventures into Freudian space with the idea that he will find the major path toward a renewal of our knowledge of mankind. By thus putting himself on the trail of what Freud pursued before him, Laplanche does not seek to "force" Freud into a univocal direction. Instead he focuses his meticulous attention on every intellectual step within psychoanalytic theory, in order to catch sight of the "false equilibria," the psychoanalytic equivalents—ingenious as they might be—of the "epicycles" and other expedients of the pre-Copernican theory.

Laplanche's telescope is therefore pointed at Freud's texts with a view to refract them—if I may extend the metaphor—through the prism of the very method developed by Freud. Such refraction disperses the whole of Freud's theorizations, which are then re-clustered around selected nodal points, only to be dispersed once again. Returning again and again to the same theorization, each time in a different context, at a different level, this approach takes the form of a spiral—or rather a helix—to borrow the image often used by Laplanche to account for the modality of his exploration of psychoanalytic theory. Let it be said that each of us in fact experiences a helicoid motion in three-dimensional space, as a result of the earth's rotation around its axis combined with its translational movement around the sun.

Laplanche's psychoanalytic work and the astronomical metaphor thus seem connected, which fits rather nicely with the fact that Laplanche regularly spent part of his summers on Samos, the island of Aristarchus, the great astronomer of ancient Greece and the first

---

2 Interview with Roland Jaccard, *Le Monde*, April 27, 1980; reprinted in *Entretiens avec Le Monde*, 5. *L'individu*. Paris: La Découverte & Le Monde, 1985.

advocate of heliocentrism. But, following Laplanche's example, I will not embark on dubious speculations about the man but will instead remain focused on the texts, the variety of which can conjure up an *n*-dimensional space.

Laplanche remains a leading figure on the international psychoanalytic scene. In the limited context of this work, I cannot undertake the long historical and theoretical digression that would be required to situate him adequately. I will therefore jump to the heart of the matter, as my point is to introduce the reader to Laplanche's most important contributions to psychoanalytic thought. All the same, it is worth mentioning that his name and ideas are featured without fail at every major crossroads of contemporary psychoanalysis, starting with the access of French readers to Freud's texts, which Laplanche was instrumental in facilitating. He was the translator of numerous texts by Freud, before and after the *The Language of Psychoanalysis*,[3] written in collaboration with J.-B. Pontalis, a book regarded as an indispensable tool in educing a rigorous mapping of Freud's concepts; it has been translated into many languages and remains an ever present reference in psychoanalytic literature. From 1988 until his death in 2012, Laplanche was also the scientific director of a colossal project: the translation of Freud's complete psychoanalytic works from the original German into French (*Œuvres psychanalytiques complètes de Freud*).[4]

General editor of two psychoanalytic book series for PUF (*Bibliothèque de psychanalyse* and *Voix nouvelles en psychanalyse*), Laplanche also founded and, for the twenty years or so of its existence, directed the journal *Psychanalyse à l'université*. As its name implies, that jour-

---

3 Laplanche J., Pontalis J.-B. (1973 [1967]). *The Language of Psycho-analysis*, Donald Nicholson-Smith, translator. The International Psycho-Analytical Library 94:1-497. London: The Hogarth Press and the Institute of Psycho-Analysis.

4 This project was undertaken with a team of tightly integrated translators (including André Bourguignon and Pierre Cotet as publishing directors) and generated shock waves and controversies regarding the intransigence of some of its choices. See *Traduire Freud*, Paris: PUF, 1987.

nal (in English, *Psychoanalysis in the University*) was closely related to another of Laplanche's major contributions, the introduction and development of university research in psychoanalysis, which I will discuss below. Laplanche was a founding member and, for some time, president of the French Psychoanalytic Association. His work was translated into many languages, and he was invited to lecture and lead seminars all over the world. He was made a knight in France's Order of Arts and Letters in 1990 and in 1995 was awarded the prestigious Sigourney Award by the American Psychoanalytic Association. His work has been the focus of numerous international conferences in countries including Canada, the U.K., and Spain.

It is impossible here to tackle all the aspects of Laplanche's work. Instead I will focus mainly on the original and rigorous theoretical developments he has bequeathed us: *original* insofar as he was able to plow a furrow in the psychoanalytic field, one that is a reopening as well as a reinstatement, to borrow one of his terms; *rigorous* insofar as it is based on a deep knowledge of Freud's texts and a consistent reliance on Freud's method.

The Discourse of the Analytic Method

To mention the "psychoanalytic scene" is naturally to summon the figure of Jacques Lacan, not so much with a view to ascertaining the relative "importance" of Lacan and Laplanche—a rather pointless if not puerile endeavor—but, from the outset, to underline the basic difference between Lacan's use of Freud's texts and the kind of work undertaken by Laplanche at the heart of the Freudian corpus. A great reader of Freud, Lacan famously called for a "return to Freud," a necessary move indeed but one that at times was more a *recourse* to Freud, reference to whom arguably provided Lacan's arguments a Freudian imprimatur. Laplanche's position is radically different: his turning *toward* Freud—a return deploying the weapons of the Freudian method—aims, in effect, at introducing a process of fundamental questioning into the heart of Freud's texts. To Laplanche, quoting Freud does not guarantee anything at all; it merely instigates thought and provides a locus for psychoanalytic work. In contrast to Lacan, Laplanche does not seek to enlist psychoanalysis under the banner of some pilot science, be it linguistics or mathematics. Nor does he seek to "pocket all of Freud's insights for his own benefit."[5] Rather, he maps out the various trends that run through Freud's work—trends at times divergent, even contradictory—without necessarily feeling compelled to choose. On the other hand, he is able to make critical choices at decisive moments, choices he always explicitly claims as his own. According to Laplanche, the point is not to establish the "true" meaning of Freud's texts, but to remain true to Freud's method, deploying it, if needed, even against Freud himself. However, this faithfulness to the Freudian method is not an end in itself: it is a matter of putting Freud's *invention* to work again, thanks to a method indissolubly tied to the analytic situation, thereby continuing the fulfillment of Freud's *exigency*, the pursuit of the object that set Freud's thought in motion: the unconscious and its realism.

In the course of this research, Laplanche teaches us how to read Freud and, in so doing, how to reflect on psychoanalysis. The foundational act consists in turning the analytic method upon the Freudian corpus itself, to let it speak for itself, to deepen the questions that have been posed, and to learn even from its ambiguities and contradictions, its hesitations and aporias. Laplanche's reading is at once literal, critical, and interpretive,[6] an approach he refers to as putting Freud's texts and concepts to work or, alternatively, as making them *sweat* or *give up the ghost*. For it is undoubtedly the spirit or the soul of psychoanalysis that Laplanche's work seeks to lay bare in an attempt to account for what impels psychoanalysis in relation to neighbor-

---

5 *L&D*, p. 5 (translation modified).
6 *L&D*, pp. 3–5.

ing fields. Yet Laplanche's project does not imply any dichotomy between body and soul. In fact, he radically rejects such a dichotomy by demonstrating that the dividing line actually runs between self-preservation and the sexual sphere, each of which includes both somatic and psychic components. His aim is to delineate and reaffirm the soul, the driving force of Freud's invention, through an initial process of decomposition applied to theory in its "unified form" (Gestalt) and an in-depth examination of the manifest discourse of Freud and his successors.

Laplanche's wish to "make Freud give up the ghost" might sound a bit aggressive, if not violent, and indeed Laplanche's critique actually involves a certain degree of violence: violence against the dogmatic satisfaction of treating Freud's texts as sacred and untouchable; violence against any form of vague theorizing that indulges in endless ad hoc hypotheses regardless of how they might fit in with the overall theoretical edifice. This is what underlies Laplanche's call for a permanent Copernican revolution in psychoanalysis, in order to oppose, first, the culture of "small differences" akin to the multiplication of ancillary mechanisms in the Ptolemaic celestial system. More fundamentally, this revolution involves a critique of the centering on ego or self that characterizes most of the dominant theories in psychoanalysis: a kind of *ipsocentrism* akin to Ptolemaic geocentrism. Let us bear in mind that the pivotal term in Freud's discovery precisely denotes a process of *de*centering similar to the process implemented by Copernicus. This second issue is the more crucial of the two: since various psychoanalytic theories are developed around the notion of an unconscious which, though it has dethroned the ego, remains located at the center of the individual, of the self (*ipse*), and has thus morphed into a familiar center; such theories are bound to produce endless concepts and mechanisms in order to compensate, as best they can, for the failure to conceptualize such a radical alien as the unconscious.

For Laplanche, reading Freud and reflecting on psychoanalysis are a single process because he reads Freud following Freud's own method, which aims not to provide a scholastic commentary on the texts but rather to introduce, within the corpus, a problematic whose development might yield major theoretical rearticulations. The point is to uncover a variety of trails to be followed as far as possible in order to find out where they lead while subjecting them, if need be, to a radical critique. On the basis of Freud's fundamental intuitions, Laplanche conceives the locus of the analytic experience as the locus of a *de*translation of the text, a necessary preamble to a process of *re*translation likely to yield a less rigid, more open version of the text.

"Interpreting [with] Freud," a somewhat programmatic essay published in 1968, is Laplanche's first account of his method.[7] The method basically consists in applying psychoanalytic work to a written text. Yet psychoanalytic work implies the implementation, outside the frame of the session, of the fundamental rule established by Freud: free association by the patient, evenly suspended attention by the analyst. But one may wonder how free association and evenly suspended attention can exist outside the consulting room. As Laplanche writes, "plowing up the corpus from all angles without omitting or privileging anything *a priori*, in our view this might well be the equivalent of the fundamental rule in the analytic treatment."[8] Through associations and cross-references, through a process of deconstruction in keeping with the original meaning of the term *analysis,* a dissolution of the text's intended form is carried out, a dissolution on the horizon of which another reality may arise.[9] In the treatment, unconscious fantasy is what that other reality consists in. In the work on Freud's texts, the unconscious fantasies of Freud-the-man or some "unconscious of the text" are not what the method leads to; what are unveiled instead are the exigencies posited by the very object of Freud's research, exi-

---

7 Laplanche, J. (2006 [1968]), "Interpreting [with] Freud." *Psychoanalysis, Culture and Society* 11:171–184.

8 "Interpreting [with] Freud," p. 179–180 (translation modified).

9 "Ponctuation," in *La révolution copernicienne inachevée*, p. xiv.

gencies that inflect the researcher's approach, imposing diversions and returns and, seemingly, even at times leading him astray. As Laplanche points out, the method is not only suited to the object; it is also directed by it, drawn by it like a magnet.[10]

Let us stress that such methodological questions are not the fussy quibbles of a "Freudologist": they are of major importance to psychoanalysis. Given the triumphalism of neuro- and cognitive science at a time when Freud's credibility and that of his successors is stridently challenged, Laplanche's decades of work provide valuable tools for mapping out the specific domain of psychoanalytic research and establishing its scientific legitimacy. Identification of the object of psychoanalysis simultaneously delineates the domain of its practitioners' proficiencies for both clinical and theoretical practice. Later I will discuss the particulars of the object and domain specific to psychoanalysis as Laplanche envisions them. Let me merely point out, for now, that Freud himself foregrounds issues of method when attempting to define psychoanalysis: primarily a *method of investigation* of otherwise inaccessible psychic phenomena, psychoanalysis is only secondarily a *psychotherapeutic method* based on that method of investigation; and, finally, it is a collection of theories resulting from the method of investigation and treatment. This insistence on method is crucial in that it safeguards psychoanalysis against any temptation to dogmatism. Defining psychoanalysis as a method implies that the theory should itself be subject to methodical work or, as Laplanche suggests, that it should be one of the sites of psychoanalytic experience.[11] Let us say, then, that Laplanche was able to gauge how psychoanalysis not only could but also needed to reexamine its foundations. Any examination of the theory of a specific era must take stock, as would be done in examining any conscious formation, of whatever may operate as an obstacle or resistance on the path of access to the unconscious.

---

10 See *Le fourvoiement biologisant de Freud*, pp.7–9.
11 The French word *expérience* means both "experience" and "experiment."

The first instances of this method's implementation are seen in two authoritative works written in collaboration with Pontalis: *The Language of Psycho-analysis,* a book which, fifty years after its publication, remains an indispensable reference for any psychoanalyst or any reader of Freud; and "Primal Fantasy, Fantasies of Origins, Origins of Fantasy."[12] In each of these texts, the examination of Freud's corpus from various angles unveiled concepts that proved crucial to an understanding of Freud's thought. In these early texts, one can discern in retrospect, either hinted at or spelled out, themes on which Laplanche was to focus in subsequent years, especially the question of *leaning-on* (*Anlehnung; anaclisis* in Strachey's translation),[13] as well as the much broader issue of the theory of seduction. Major later works elaborated these issues, first narrowing the focus of investigation and then relaunching it within the context of a more open exploration. Published in 1970, *Life and Death in Psychoanalysis* can be seen as providing a condensed, definitive take on the issue of leaning-on, a narrowing of focus following the wide-ranging examination of Freud's texts necessitated by *The Language of Psycho-analysis.* After *Life and Death,* Laplanche set about broadening his research in the context of his teaching in the university. In no apparent order, he explored various *Problématiques,*[14] until he narrowed his focus again in

---

12 Translator's note: The French original, "Fantasme originaire, fantasme des origines, origine du fantasme," was first published in *Les Temps modernes* (1964) and then reprinted with a new introduction by the authors in 1985 (Hachette). An English translation was published in 1968 in the *International Journal of Psychoanalysis* 49 and a new translation of the 1985 version is published in the volume.

13 Translator's note: The English translation of Freud's term *Anlehnung* has been the subject of some debate. Strachey opts for "anaclisis" in the *Standard Edition.* "Leaning-on" and "propping" are other available translations. While Laplanche himself favored the use of "leaning-on," Jeffrey Mehlman, in his translation of *Life and Death in Psychoanalysis,* used "propping" for the noun (a translation of the French word *étayage*) and "to prop oneself upon" for the verbal form.

14 *Problématiques* refers to a series of seminars taught by Laplanche. Initially only five volumes containing the seminars given from 1980 to 1987 were published with that title. Later two more series of seminars were given the titles *Problématiques VI* and *Problématiques VII.* All are listed in the bibliography.

1987, with the publication of *New Foundations for Psychoanalysis*. Following this pivotal text, Laplanche's research and reflection ranged over a variety of other topics. The subsequent publication of *La révolution copernicienne inachevée* (*The Unfinished Copernican Revolution*) is a good illustration of the spiraling motion invoked by Laplanche when accounting for the development of his thought: often running vertically through the same points, yet shifting the issue with every new turn of the spiral. Written many years after "Interpreting [with] Freud," it features Laplanche's debate with hermeneutics, a debate that in fact dates back to 1960, in a paper he presented (in collaboration with Serge Leclaire) at the Bonneval Conference: "The Unconscious: A Psychoanalytic Study."

Incidentally, that 1960 paper illustrates an aspect of Laplanche's work relating directly to my comments about method: Laplanche shows that one can take on a theoretical legacy without being trapped by it and without having to renounce one's own line of thinking. In view of this, let us recall that Laplanche was analyzed by Lacan and was among his most brilliant students. During the historic conference at Bonneval, Laplanche arguably represented, along with his friend Leclaire, a theoretical trend associated with Lacan. All the same, Laplanche was already able to carve out a theoretical position distinct from that of his erstwhile master and to pursue his own original research. Although initially he and Leclaire relied on tools borrowed by Lacan from Saussurean linguistics, in the sections of the paper that Laplanche wrote himself, he embarked on a most personal reflection, differentiating himself from Lacan, for whom the unconscious is structured like a language. Lacan's case for a homology between language and the unconscious is criticized unequivocally by Laplanche in terms that show a full allegiance to Freud. Section IV, which follows Leclaire's contribution, is titled "The Unconscious Is the Condition for Language: Interdependence of Preconscious and Unconscious Systems." There Laplanche writes, straightaway, "The preceding analysis [that of the 'unicorn dream' presented and analyzed by Leclaire] leads us, as Lacan has shown, to identify what Freud calls primary process—the free flow of libidinal energy along paths of displacement and condensation—with the fundamental laws of linguistics. Were we to stop at this all too simple conception, however, we would run up against the most serious objections, and it is in Freud himself that we find them set out most clearly."[15] Laplanche offers a summary of Freud's views on the relationship between language and psychic topography and stresses that language that functions in accordance with primary process is not language in general but the language of schizophrenics. He argues: "Let us indicate at once the idea which will govern the rest of our discussion: [the] ballast which removes language from the exclusive domination of the primary process . . . [is] precisely the existence of the unconscious chain."[16] A classic text that remains most relevant today, "The Unconscious: A Psychoanalytic Study" also features a preliminary sketch of some of the great forthcoming axes in Laplanche's theorizing: primal repression, the constitution of the unconscious, the realism of the unconscious.

Life and Death: The Sexual in Psychoanalysis

Despite its undeniable rigor, the 1960 paper on the unconscious is restricted to a rather formal approach, due certainly to the influence of the linguistic and structural model introduced by Lacan. When considering the main arguments advanced in the Bonneval presentation in the light of Laplanche's subsequent thought, one is struck that while appropriate attention is given to unconscious and preconscious mechanisms and their relation to language, the sexual unconscious is hardly brought into play. By contrast, ten years later, in *Life and Death in Psychoanalysis*, the sexual has become central.

---

15 J. Laplanche & S. Leclaire, "The Unconscious: A Psychoanalytic Study," *French Yale Studies* 48, 1972, p. 151.
16 *Ibid.*, p. 152.

To grasp the relevance of a text, one must locate it in the context of its production. The Bonneval paper was inscribed in a controversy over the "narrativist" position of the French Communist philosopher Georges Politzer. In brief, that position was that the unconscious is essentially a *meaning* from which one is temporarily alienated and that must be assumed in the first person. Politzer's position leads to a critique of Freud's metapsychology, which Politzer reproved both on the grounds of its abstraction—the abstraction of mechanisms compared with the first-person assumption of unconscious discourse—and on the grounds of its realism as opposed to a kind of constructivism (which, incidentally, would seem quite akin to Freud's position in "Constructions in Analysis"). No doubt Politzer's critique warranted Laplanche's insistence on issues of forms and mechanisms. Yet if, in comparison, *Life and Death in Psychoanalysis* offers a shift in focus, by aiming to "retrace the vicissitude of the vital order (life and death) when it is transposed to the level of the psychic apparatus"—"this transformation into something different that life undergoes when it symbolizes itself on the human level"[17]—it also continues the exploration of the foundations of psychic life and, ultimately, the specificity and reality of the unconscious.

The Origin of the Sexual in Psychic Life

Life and Death is a text that has had a momentous impact on psychoanalytic thought in France, as well as in the Anglo-American tradition. Yet it was called into question by Laplanche himself, especially with regard to the notion of leaning-on, prominently developed in this book. The reasons for this reexamination will be explored, but to understand them properly one must have a good grasp of Laplanche's thought at the time. Let me point out in passing that,

---

17 *L&D*, p. 7

for many, *Life and Death* is not truly challenged by Laplanche's subsequent reformulations, which are seen as extensions of rather than a departure from the 1970 book.[18]

The chapters of *Life and Death* draw a curve from the vital order's relation with the genesis of sexuality to a questioning of the death drive's function in the general structure of Freud's texts. Laplanche raises the following questions: While Freudian psychoanalysis is obviously contiguous with biology, can it be reduced to biology? If not, how is the field of psychoanalysis organized in relation to the basic notions operating at its borders: life and death?

Starting from *Three Essays on the Theory of Sexuality*, Laplanche first specifies the role of the vital order and its relation to sexuality. Laplanche uses the concept of leaning-on, which runs through all the chapters, to show the derivation of the sexual from the vital, adaptational sphere. This derivation, subsequently criticized by Laplanche, sets up a clear distinction between the two domains, which Freud himself tends to conflate in some of his writings. Following the sequence of themes in *Three Essays*, Laplanche articulates a movement in Freud's thought that "follows—as in every profound exercise of thought—the movement of the 'thing itself'."[19] Laplanche suggests that the essay on "sexual aberrations" be subtitled "The Instinct Lost": the point is to defeat any argument that might lead to a conflation of sexual drive and instinct. In demonstrating the variability of human sexuality, perversions show how the sexual drive differs from instinct, notably in its deviations with regard to aim and object. The aim of an instinct is basically adaptational: feeding, defending one's territory, reproducing. The aim of the drive is basically satisfaction. The objects of the instinct are relatively fixed (e.g., food, intruders to be repelled). By contrast, the objects of the sexual drive are infinitely varied: the only requirement is that they contribute to satisfaction. Perversions specifically reveal

---

18 See, e.g., J. Mehlman, "Verweile doch! Pour l'étayage," in J. Laplanche et al., *Colloque international de psychanalyse*, PUF, 1994, pp. 79–86.
19 *L&D*, p. 9.

the contingency of sexual objects and in so doing break the homology between drives and instincts. When it comes to perversions, Freud's intention is not to describe some accidental deviation of instinct. On the contrary, as Laplanche clearly demonstrates, his point is to ascertain how human sexuality as a whole can be conceived of as deviant.

The well-known example used by Freud is that of the child sucking at the breast after hunger has subsided. This is how Laplanche's reading of Freud in *Life and Death* may be summarized: leaning on what started out as the exercise of a basic nutritive function, there arises an infantile sexual activity predicated on the formation of an erotogenic zone. This may seem like a simple scene, but it contains complex phenomena. Activity that, strictly speaking, is instinctual (self-preservative) is directed from the outset toward an object in the external world, and this object is at once vital and specific insofar as it is essential to the organism's survival. The formation of the erotogenic zone, by way of derivation, signals a regression with respect to the original relation with the external world: the object of need (milk in this case) is lost sight of and overshadowed by the metonymic (contiguous) object that is constituted by the breast in its erotogenic relation with the labial zone. From this point on, the breast itself becomes contingent, likely to be replaced by anything endowed with the property of stimulating the labial zone, which by now has become the locus of satisfaction of the oral sexual drive. First serving a vital function, the mouth morphs into an organ of erotogenic pleasure, a sort of pleasure destined subsequently to acquire even greater independence in relation to the external object by becoming *autoerotic*. In this way, a relatively fixed object of need—milk—leads to the breast, an already contingent sexual object that in a process of autoerotic regression gives way to the fantasized object: "Thus leaning-on consists initially in that support which emergent sexuality finds in a function linked to the preservation of life."[20]

---

20 *L&D*, p. 17 (translation modified).

Laplanche points to the issue that arises in analytic theory as soon as autoerotism is brought into play. Many, including Freud himself at times, have viewed autoerotism as an entirely "anobjectal" state, raising the related issue of how, one day, an object manages to appear. Such a line of thinking has led certain authors to go so far as to posit a "normal autism" in every child. Others, following Freud, have made a case for a state of "absolute primary narcissism," without demonstrating how the child could emerge from such a state. Conversely, some have argued that the object is present from the beginning. From Balint's "primary object love" to Fairbairn's claim that the drive is primarily object-seeking—in other words, that the drive possesses a kind of foreknowledge of the object—theories have been elaborated in an attempt to surmise, via an a priori posit, the child's necessary emergence from the anobjectal state posited by others. But these contrasted positions are in fact complementary insofar as the correction of one by the other is generally predicated on a confusion between the object of need and the sexual object.

This is a typical example of the "Ptolemaic" complexification of psychoanalysis through theories which, because they overlook fundamental aspects, are forced to find a new equilibrium by resorting to theoretical expedients akin to the ingenious epicycles devised to account for the apparent wanderings of planets. This is where Laplanche's reading of Freud intervenes as a third term in the prevailing false dichotomy between "no object at all" and a sexual object present from the beginning. The methodical reading of *Three Essays* with a focus on the key notion of leaning-on permits Laplanche to "slip the knife" into notions that are less coherent and solid than they seem. For this purpose, one must first read the *whole* text so as to then discern the various steps, the displacements within the corpus under study. This is how, in the third essay, Laplanche finds the material required to escape the aporia that could doom the concept of leaning-on, as a result of its reference to autoerotism. Laplanche first quotes the text of the third essay: "At a time at which the beginnings of sexual satisfaction are still linked with the taking of nourishment [i.e., at the time of the process of leaning-on], the sexual drive has a sexual object outside the infant's own body in the shape of his mother's breast. It is only later that he loses it, just at the time, perhaps, when he is able to form a total representation of the person to whom the organ that is giving him satisfaction belongs. As a rule the sexual drive then becomes auto-erotic [thus autoerotism is not the initial stage], and not until the period of latency has been passed through is the original relation restored. There are thus good reasons why a child sucking at his mother's breast has become the prototype of every relation of love. The finding of an object is in fact a re-finding of it."[21]

Laplanche's reading of the above section is as follows: "if such a text is to be taken seriously, it means that *on the one hand there is an object from the beginning, but that on the other hand sexuality does not have a real object from the beginning*. It should be understood that the real object, milk, was the object of the function, which is virtually pre-ordained to the world of satisfaction. Such is the real object which has been lost, but the object linked to the autoerotic retrogression, the breast—which has become a fantasized breast—is, for its part, the object of the sexual drive. Thus the sexual object is not identical to the object of the function . . . [T]he object to be recovered is not the lost object, but its substitute by displacement; the lost object is the object of self-preservation, of hunger, and the object one seeks to refind in sexuality is an object displaced in relation to that first object. From this, of course, arises the impossibility of ultimately ever rediscovering the object, since the object which has been lost is *not the same* as that which is to be rediscovered. Therein lies the key to the essential 'duplicity' situated at the very beginning of the sexual quest."[22] The false dilemma of an anobjectal autoerotic state (in contradiction

---

21 S. Freud, *Three Essays on the Theory of Sexuality*, SE VII, p. 222 (*GW* V, p. 123), quoted by Laplanche in *Life and Death*, p. 19. Laplanche's comments are in brackets (translation modified).
22 *L&D*, pp. 19–20 (translation modified).

with the very idea of a quest for the lost object) versus an erotic object present from the outset (leveling the distinction between drive and instinct) thus finds its resolution. For this to happen, Freud's thought had to be dissected, the knife slipped into what Freud refers to as a sexual object located outside the subject's own body in order to distinguish between the satisfaction of the need for nourishment, on the one hand, and, on the other, a "sexuality [that] draws away from its natural object, finds itself delivered over to fantasy and in this very process is constituted *qua* sexuality."[23] The latter formulation is taken from *The Language of Psycho-analysis*, not from *Life and Death*; I chose to quote it because it epitomizes what Laplanche will himself later criticize in his own reading of Freud. If leaning-on indeed elicits the delineation of two distinct fields, an essential stage in the identification of the specific object of psychoanalysis, it nonetheless appears as conducive to a view of the sexual sphere and its origin that could easily be subsumed within the instinctual domain, despite having just been distinguished from it. Such a risk is not hypothetical: Laplanche will subsequently show how, at some point, Freud himself reinstinctualizes the sexual sphere.

The Limitations of Leaning-on

Five years after writing *Life and Death,* Laplanche returned to his reading of Freud regarding the theory of leaning-on. The radical moment in the critique of this theory takes place during his lecture on December 16, 1975, which ends with the following statement: "The theory of seduction is even more important than the theory of leaning-on or, if you prefer, it is the theory of seduction that carries the truth of leaning-on."[24] In *The Temptation of Biology: Freud's Theories of*

---

23 J. Laplanche & J.-B. Pontalis, *The Language of Psycho-analysis, op. cit.,* "Auto-erotism," p. 46.
24 *P3*, p. 69

Sexuality,[25] a book written after the introduction of the general theory of seduction, Laplanche resumes his harsh critique of leaning-on and the questioning of his own 1970 reading. "It must be acknowledged," Laplanche writes in 1992, "that when Pontalis and I wrote in the entry on autoerotism in *The Language of Psycho-Analysis,* and when I reiterated, in what I have since written about leaning-on, that autoerotism is bound to fantasy, we were talking about what we would like Freud to have said, though he did not. The fact is that for Freud autoerotism means 'completely without an object,' whether external to one's own body or fantasized: lacking any external object, even an object that is 'external' in fantasy."[26] Such an amendment is unsettling, but its origin will be clarified once I tackle *New Foundations for Psychoanalysis.* For the time being though, let us stress Laplanche's exemplary capacity to reconsider his positions when the pursuit of his research requires it. If this reconsideration was at first disconcerting for those who had followed Laplanche up to that point, it opened up the possibility of debate and a space for personal research in ways that few psychoanalytic authors, apart from Freud, are able to provide.

It is true that even in *Life and Death in Psychoanalysis* Laplanche stresses how leaning-on cannot adequately account for the genesis of sexuality from the vital order. This conceptual deficiency stems from several limiting factors: the characterization of the vital order, the temporal sequence of events, and the factors triggering the events in question. Let us start with the third limiting factor. In itself, leaning-on gives the impression that sexuality *arises* from self-preservative situations a bit as the flower blossoms forth from the bud. The theory of leaning-on seems to imply that if an instinctual adaptive function persists long enough, the sexual sphere will kick in. The general mechanism that Freud invokes here consists in libidinal coexcitation, according to which anything significant occurring in the body

---

25 Laplanche J, (2015 [1993]). *The Temptation of Biology: Freud's Theories of Sexuality,* Donald Nicholson-Smith, translator.
26 *op. cit.* p. 40.

necessarily leads to sexual excitation. Thus, once a certain qualitative threshold has been crossed, the vital order appears as the source of the sexual order. It consequently becomes hard to distinguish sexuality as a field clearly distinct from self-preservation because one is the natural extension of the other. This is where the second limiting factor invoked by Laplanche comes into play: the temporal sequence. When described "naturalistically," as Freud does, the temporality of leaning-on appears in a linear form that can give the impression that the sexual simply arises from self-preservation. But this approach fails to take into account the position from which we describe the facts.

We indeed overlook the fact that the observer is already completely immersed in a sexual world—a sexuality that is largely repressed—and it is on this basis that self-preservation is observed and described. Hence the insoluble illusion of a continuous process between the self-preservative and the sexual spheres. "Therein lies the whole problem of the 'vital order' in man and of the possibility, or rather the impossibility, of grasping it 'beneath' what has come to 'cover' it (assuming that these terms still have any other than a strictly didactic function)."[27] Our view of self-preservation is thus necessarily *compromised*—compromised understood in the sense Laplanche later gives it, that is to say: compromised by the unconscious. Such a view, in hindsight, prevents any truly linear description of the course of events in the process of leaning-on. This leads us, following our reverse path, to the first of the three limiting factors underlying the perceived deficiency of leaning-on: namely, the fact that leaning-on would come into being merely on account of an inherently deficient, dehiscent self-preservative sphere. But while such an explanation might appear to be satisfying (the sexual takes over for a deficient vital process), what seemingly emerges is in fact disqualified by the very deficiency of self-preservation. The debility of self-preservation cannot logically be seen as begetting, by itself, something stronger

---

27 *L&D*, p. 25.

than it is. Such debility implies the intervention of an other from the outset, this helping other (*nebenmensch*) described by Freud as early as 1895, in the *Project for a Scientific Psychology.*

Reopening the Theory of Seduction

Starting with the second chapter of *Life and Death,* Laplanche can be seen taking a first step beyond the theory of leaning-on and shifting in the direction of a theory of seduction. While on the one hand sexuality seems to emerge suddenly from the vital processes by means of deviation or derivation, on the other it is *"implanted* in the child from the parental universe: from its structures, meanings, and fantasies."[28] I will revisit this development insofar as it is featured and unfurled more broadly in another key book by Laplanche, namely, *New Foundations for Psychoanalysis.* For the time being let us simply note that what will be proposed as the *general theory of seduction* seventeen years later is rooted in this 1970 book in which Laplanche examines texts featuring pivotal elements in Freud's thought.

Hailed by Freud in 1896 as the equivalent—as regards hysteria—of the discovery of a source of the Nile, and then hastily (and secretly) dismissed by him the following year, at first sight the theory of seduction seems rather simple, if not simplistic: in childhood the hysteric (such is Freud's apparent contention) was sexually abused by an adult. Freud's assertion was based on revelations made to him by some of his patients diagnosed as hysterics. During the 1980s, this theory and Freud's abandonment of it were discussed at length when Jeffrey Masson caused a so-called scandal by accusing Freud of having cowardly abandoned his 1896 theory out of concern for respectability or sheer careerism.[29] The debate was then centered on

---

28 *L&D,* p. 48.
29 J. Masson, *The Assault on Truth: Freud's Suppression of the Seduction Theory.* New York: Farrar, Straus & Giroux, 1984.

the following opposition: truthful facts vs. mere hysterical fantasies. This debate is still rife, especially in the U.S., where two factions are violently opposed: a group of therapists and patients, on the one hand, who posit that an actual case of sexual abuse almost always premises a psychopathological case (and suggest that cases of sexual abuse are growing exponentially, sometimes described in extravagant forms) vs. advocates of "false memory syndrome."[30]

That new either/or dichotomy sorely lacks the methodical reading of a Laplanche. As he points out in *Life and Death,* "In Freud's thought, seduction may be situated in two different registers: on the one hand, it is a *clinical observation,* which is successively affirmed, refuted, called into question, and once again reaffirmed through Freud's final texts; on the other hand, it is a *theory* elaborated on the basis of that observation of the fact(s) of seduction."[31] Yet while Freud's abandonment of the seduction theory has been celebrated as the advent of the specific object of psychoanalysis (i.e., unconscious fantasy), what has been overlooked is the nature of the alternative that most often results from reducing the domain of fantasy to a simple imaginary vs. "actual facts." This dichotomy, having not been subjected to a systematic critique and having been left to its own devices, has undergone a monstrous development on the American continent, yielding the two positions I have just mentioned. We see how insubstantial the resulting positions are, as evidenced, for example, by the fact that the position that originally claimed to be the most realistic one (seduction as a fact that necessarily occurs in reality) has lapsed into the most fantastical stories: "satanic rituals" have reportedly become common practice in quiet American suburbs and towns, rituals involving the rape of children, cannibalism, alien abduction, and rape in flying saucers. Conversely, the view of fantasy as "pure imagination" ("false memory") has seemingly become the most realistic version!

---

30 For an overview of this phenomenon, see I. Hacking, *Rewriting the Soul: Multiple Personality and the Sciences of Memory.* Princeton: Princeton University Press, 1995.
31 *L&D,* p. 31.

What is lost sight of here, despite Laplanche's constant insistence, is the fact that in Freud the *theory* of seduction cannot be reduced to this false dichotomy. In the second chapter of *Life and Death in Psychoanalysis,* Laplanche takes a close look at Freud's account of trauma and memory in the *Project for a Scientific Psychology,* that is to say, the theory of the hysterical *proton pseudos,* or "first lie." "Hysterics tend to lie, as is known and as was by no means unknown before Freud. . . . With the term *proton pseudos,* however, something other than a subjective lie is being invoked; at stake is a transition from the subjective to a foundational—perhaps even to a transcendental dimension—in any event a kind of objective lie inscribed in the facts."[32] A little further on Laplanche continues: "From its inception, definitively, psychoanalysis thus maintained itself beyond the banalities of official 'clinical' practice, which regularly invoked bad faith and simulation to account for what it called 'pithiatism'. If hysterics lie, they are above all the first victims of a kind of lie or deception. Not that they have been lied to; it is rather as though there existed in the facts themselves a kind of fundamental duplicity for which we would propose the term *fallacy.* 'Primal fallacy': perhaps such is our best translation of the *proton pseudos* in its specificity."[33] How should this "objective lie, inscribed in facts" be read, and what are the "facts" in question? Could this imply a return to the "actual facts" championed by one faction in the aforementioned American dichotomy?

Laplanche's patient exploration of Freud's text yields a situation dramatically different from the one suggested by the reference to "facts." The facts at stake are psychic facts whose mechanics are bound to appear unsettling to anyone claiming to reduce Freud's theory to a linear form. Indeed, Freud makes this clear in his account of the case of Emma, a patient for whom trauma develops in two distinct stages:

---

32 *L&D*, pp. 33–34, *passim* (translation modified).
33 *Ibid.* (translation modified). Mikkel Borch-Jacobsen might benefit from pondering this excerpt, in my opinion, in view of his *Remembering Anna O.: A Century of Mystification,* transl. Kirby Olson. London: Routledge, 1996.

in the first stage, an actual sexual assault is perpetrated on an eight-year-old girl, an event that in itself has no traumatic effect. "A scene, then," Laplanche writes, "which has no immediate sexual effect, produces no excitation, and provokes no defense; and the term Freud uses to characterize it effectively conveys this ambiguous or even contradictory quality: the scene is said to be 'sexual-presexual'."[34]

Laplanche then shows how the second scene, which occurred shortly after the young girl reached puberty, is equally devoid of sexuality, even though it triggers the patient's panic and phobia. It is a rather trivial scene during which two shop-assistants laugh together. The scene, insignificant in itself, reactivates the memory of the first scene and it is this *memory* that becomes traumatic, triggering a sexual reaction made possible by sexual maturation on the one hand and, on the other, by the set of sexual representations or meanings now available to Emma. A trauma thus results from a series of events, or of scenes, neither of which is traumatic in itself. Laplanche remarks that "we never manage to fix the traumatic event historically. This fact might be illustrated by the image of a Heisenberg-like 'relation of indeterminacy': in situating the trauma, one cannot appreciate its traumatic impact, and *vice versa.*"[35] Compared to the dichotomous rift between advocates of "actual facts" and advocates of "false memories," the relation of indeterminacy emphasized by Laplanche paves the way for a scene that is much fuller in potentialities and in which, notably and in full alignment with Freud's logic, the dynamics of the unconscious may be grasped as far more than a mere stockroom of memories. This leads to an affirmation of the particular form of psychic temporality featuring après-coup,[36] as established by Freud,

---

34 *L&D*, p. 40.

35 *L&D*, p. 41.

36 Translator's note: Following editorial guidelines, the term *après-coup* is used consistently throughout this text to translate the German *Nachträglichkeit* (Strachey's "deferred action" in the *Standard Edition*), despite Laplanche's preference for the neologism "afterwardsness," which he coined (see "Notes on Afterwardsness").

brought to light by Lacan, and providing, thanks to Laplanche, a few further theoretical perspectives. I have paid special attention to this rather classic moment in Freud's theorization because it establishes a kind of platform from which the most decisive aspect of Laplanche's research proceeds.

From Après-coup to Origin

The particular twofold structure of trauma, featuring *après-coup*, is specifically related to human sexuality, which is uniquely suspended between "too soon" and "too late": the "too late" of physiological maturation, which fails to provide, in timely fashion, the answers the child needs to understand and integrate the sexual scenes; yet "too soon" insofar as sexuality, in its various scenes, is brought in to the child precociously, from the adult world, from without. Following Freud, what is at stake here is precisely the *theory* of seduction, namely how the question of the origin of sexuality can be answered. This also relativizes the importance of the effective "scenes" whose actuality Freud never stopped upholding, but which ultimately he located in a general model featuring innocuous "facts": indeed, Freud sees in ordinary maternal care an unavoidable seduction of the child by the adult. Early seduction at the hands of a mother who in spite of herself happens to be a seducer, such is the truth of leaning-on, a process which, following Laplanche, as we have seen, fails to account for the origin of sexuality: "Such care, in focusing on certain bodily regions, contributes to *defining* them as erotogenic zones, zones of exchange, which demand and provoke excitation in order subsequently to reproduce it autonomously, through *internal* stimulation."[37] But then Laplanche immediately takes a step further, continuing his ongoing critique of leaning-on and making a first breakthrough

---

37 *L&D*, p. 44.

toward a theory of *primal* seduction: "But here, we should go a step further and not restrict ourselves to the pure materiality of stimulating actions, if indeed such 'materiality' can ever be conceived of in isolation. We should, in fact, consider that beyond the contingency and transiency of any specific experience, it is the intrusion into the universe of the child of certain meanings of the adult world which is conveyed by the most ordinary and innocent of acts. The whole of the primal intersubjective relation—between mother and child—is saturated with these meanings."[38] Such views lead Laplanche to a reinterpretation, a few paragraphs later, of the theory of the *proton pseudos* examined in detail at the beginning of the same chapter. What Freud describes as an event must, on this theory, be understood as a sort of *implantation*[39] of sexuality in the child. Thus reinterpreted it emerges not as any lived or datable trauma but "as a factor which is both more diffuse and more structural, a more *primal* factor as well in the sense that it is so linked to the process of humanization that it is only through abstraction that we can suppose the existence of a small child 'before' that seduction."[40]

Primal: the word is out, pointing to the dimension of seduction that lies beyond common temporality, beyond events, without becoming less real or effective in any way. What is primal, however, is *not* what is at the beginning; at stake is the relation of indeterminacy between the two stages of trauma described by Freud. What is primal is what lies at the bottom, at the foundations. This introduces a kind of transcendence: what originally presented itself as a special case, as a pathogenic event—sexual trauma resulting from a perverse adult attacking an innocent child—is thus superseded (in the sense of Hegel's *aufhebung* [i.e., abolished and preserved at once]) in a movement toward a general view of the adult-child relation in which

---

38 *Ibid.*
39 As I will discuss, Laplanche resorts to the term "implantation" more systematically later on.
40 *L&D*, p. 46. Italics mine.

sexual "meanings" are grafted onto the most ordinary forms of care or exchange. The full extent of such a reinterpretation of seduction will become clear when Laplanche further develops it a few years later, granting it a central role in *New Foundations for Psychoanalysis*.

The Duality of the Ego...

Let us explore Laplanche's ideas in *Life and Death* a little further. As I have explained, Laplanche elaborated an initial theoretical generalization by slipping the knife into Freud's seduction theory, by distinguishing clinical observation from theorization per se. There, where Freud aimed to account for the etiology of hysteria in the context of a limited theory, Laplanche is able to foreground a more general theory that had been implicit. Freud's *proton pseudos* and his elaboration of the twofold temporality of trauma shift the object of psychoanalytic theorizing from hysteria to the origin of human sexuality. The outcome of this theorization is a view of memories (or *reminiscences*, to use Freud's term) operating as an "internal foreign body" that attacks from within and triggers sexual excitation. Laplanche stresses that, for Freud, this view is pivotal as it accounts for the specifically sexual dimension of the unconscious. Freud always holds the sexual as the repressed par excellence. In the texts that Laplanche puts to work before our eyes, the reason is evident: to Freud, only the sexual domain possesses the attribute of unfurling according to two phases in the course of life and of constituting, by way of reminiscences, an internal foreign body, an ever active assailant. The sexual thus plays a leading role in the modality of the attack, and thus of the conflict. This immediately raises the question of the nature of the other party involved in psychic conflict. Laplanche shows that, though there is a tendency in Freud to locate the conflict between self-preservation and sexuality (in view of the duality between these two terms), this is never what happens in the clinical studies to which it is supposed to apply. It is the ego that is being attacked by unconscious sexuality, and the ego develops defenses as a result, which is well in line with what we have previously seen regarding leaning-on.

Indeed, in the theory of leaning-on, self-preservation is posited as relatively deficient. I have pointed out how difficult it is to isolate self-preservation in humans insofar as, from the outset, the sexual order overlies the vital order. In fact, we can take things a bit further: the sexual not only leans on self-preservation (within a temporality that pertains to the primal), it buttresses the deficient self-perservative order. Where instinct proves deficient in ensuring survival of the human child, *love* takes over: love, that is, the sexual, but a sexual endowed with a metapsychological status defined by its link to the ego. Two sexual regimes are thus opposed in psychic conflict: a regime representative of the internal foreign body operating as an internal assailant (the implanted sexual) and another regime representative of the *quiescent* libidinal investment, to use Freud's term, in the service of a relatively stable structure: the ego.

The question of the ego is the focus of the next two chapters of *Life and Death in Psychoanalysis*. Coming to terms with the consequences of the theory of leaning-on, Laplanche furthers his understanding of what the pole of life might entail within the dramatic pair featured in the title of his book. If for human beings life cannot rely on self-preservative instincts, how does the vital order become endowed with any form of efficacy on the psychic scene? This issue shifts Laplanche's speculations in the direction of the ego, another illustration of Laplanche's method. Laplanche reminds us that the term *ego*, in Freud's texts, is usually understood in two distinct ways: either as referring to the whole organism, the biological individual, or as pointing to a specialized part of this biological individual (the ego as an agency). "If we want to attribute to facts of language," he writes, "a value which is not 'purely verbal', if we believe that it is never for nothing that the *same* word is used to designate two apparently different things, is not the whole problem in the relation between the two 'meanings' of the same word, and must we not account for the fact that they are used in such different contexts?"[41] Laplanche then explains the relations of derivation that operate between the concepts (from ego-as-individual to ego-as-agency) and doubles up the derivation, which is then carried out within reality itself.[42]

Derivation *by contiguity* (metonymical derivation): this refers to the process of differentiation or specialization, within a totality and in contact with reality, of an agency charged with specific functions. Such a metonymic view of the ego is representative of the dominant theoretical trend, especially as a result of American ego psychology, but it can actually be traced back to Freud: it consists in the ego-as-agency, the part differentiated in Freud's second tripartite model, id/ego/superego.

Derivation *by resemblance* (metaphorical derivation): Laplanche points out that this is the domain of identification but, before discussing the matter in these terms, he closely surveys this view of the development of the ego "by resemblance." Starting with the 1895 *Project for a Scientific Psychology,* which Laplanche describes as a "great text on the ego," the ego is introduced not in terms of its perception-related function (as is the case of the ego-as-agency, especially in the texts written in the 1920s), but in terms of its fundamentally inhibiting function. The ego is not endowed with any privileged access to reality; its task, rather, is to do away with any "excess of reality" (the outcome of internal excitation) in order to allow the indication of reality arising from external perception to penetrate.

As we know, in this 1895 text, the ego, thus constituted as a system of "well-facilitated" mnemic traces, fulfills, for Freud, its essentially inhibiting function. Because it is a stable organization, the ego is able to introduce a certain ballast, a process of binding apt to prevent the kind of free circulation typical of primary process. Thus

---

41 *L&D*, p. 50.
42 The notion of derivation is clarified by Laplanche in a short text titled "The Derivation of Psychoanalytic Entities," written as an homage to Jean Hyppolite, his mentor in philosophy, and printed as an appendix in *L&D*, pp. 127–139.

we can see the emergence of the ego as resistance and the importance of the concept of resistance in Freud's later views. This is reminiscent, not without a hint of irony in view of the currently dominant scientism, of a remark by Gaston Bachelard: "Psychology itself would become scientific if, like physics, it became discursive, if it realized that both within us and outside us, we understand nature by resisting it. From our point of view, the only legitimate intuition in psychology is the intuition of an inhibition."[43]

Next on the agenda is "On Narcissism: An Introduction." I wondered earlier how, if self-preservation is deemed deficient, the pole of life might affirm itself a psychic life. My answer was that the vital order would in turn lean on the sexual order, but the sexual in this case is characterized by its link to the ego. Laplanche's survey of the *Project* revealed the essential binding and inhibiting function of the ego, which is perfectly in accord with the ego of the 1914 essay on narcissism. In Laplanche's view, in fact, Freud upholds the thesis that narcissism is a libidinal investment of the ego. While this libidinal investment is inseparable from the process of formation of the ego, at the same time it participates in the libidinal investment of the *self*. It is to be noted that the concept of narcissism weaves together of the two derivations—metonymic and metaphoric—of the ego: the libidinal investment of the ego constitutes this differentiated and relatively stable organization, and it is this that permits the process of libidinal investment of the self (self-love) as it consists in the investment of a self-image, the image of the individual as a totality. By linking the two derivations of the ego around a common point, narcissism thus guarantees the deputization (*vicariance*) of the deficient self-preservative order.

As Laplanche stresses, however, the line of thought characterizing "On Narcissism: An Introduction" is only intermittently

---

43 G. Bachelard, *The Formation of the Scientific Mind*. Transl. by M. McAllester Jones. Paul & Company Pub Consortium, 2002, p. 33.

dominant in Freud's corpus. Indeed, "primary" or "primal" narcissism most often refers to a hypothetical original state in which the organism forms a self-enclosed unit. Such a definition raises more than one serious issue, especially the question of how it is possible to exit this state of self-sufficiency. This is something Freud seems well aware of and, as early as 1911, in a footnote to "Formulations on the Two Principles of Mental Functioning," he wonders how such an organism could keep itself alive even for the shortest time.[44] Laplanche offers a very concise discussion of this issue, which goes back to the question of the hallucinatory satisfaction of desire. On the basis of his development of the notion of autoerotism in the preceding chapters of *Life and Death*, he demonstrates how the view of narcissism expounded in Freud's 1914 text is actually at odds with what is usually dominant in Freud. In this text, narcissism is the initial state not of the whole organism but of the ego. Since, as I have noted, the narcissistic libidinal investment also constitutes the founding of the ego, the latter arises from the merging of the various zones where the kind of "on the spot" satisfaction typical of autoerotism used to operate.

. . . and the Place of the Death Drive

The question of narcissism is crucial to Laplanche because it is there, rather than in *Beyond the Pleasure Principle*, that he locates the true turning point in Freud's thinking. This turning point seems to have been repressed immediately by Freud himself when, after the introduction of narcissism, he started writing the metapsychology papers, seemingly without taking full stock of the impact of his new theorization. Yet by positing the existence of a quiescent regime of libido within the ego, narcissism reveals precisely the modalities fol-

---

44 S. Freud, "Formulations on the Two Principles of Mental Functioning," *SE* XII, p. 219.

lowing which the sexual relays self-preservation to ensure survival of the individual organism. Laplanche signals, however, that Freud is prone to some serious theoretical wavering on this subject. Under the generic term *libido*, Freud ends up conflating the sexual as "assailant" with the narcissistic libido: these two sharply contrasted libidinal regimes are thus merged under the aegis of Eros. Nonetheless, Freud is later forced, led as always by the exigency of his object, to restore a fundamental equilibrium by positing the death drive opposite Eros. According to Laplanche, the death drive and the life drives seemingly entail a reinstinctualization of the drives, especially in the light of Freud's growing reliance on the biological domain, as against the distinction established by Freud between drives and instincts.

Regarding the death drive, Laplanche's intention "is not so much to pose abstractly the question of the validity of the concept as to locate its place within the general economy of Freud's thought and, if possible, in both its diachronic and synchronic dimensions."[45] The position that arises from Laplanche's reading of the death drive is not supported unanimously.[46] Yet Laplanche's investigation of the concepts pertaining to the issue of the death drive—an investigation that encompasses the entirety of Freud's work—remains rather convincing. Laplanche foregrounds the exigency, the compulsion, the *Zwang*, that leads Freud to such an unsettling concept—a concept Laplanche strives to discuss both as the return/rediscovery of the demonic aspect of the sexual drive and as something more than a mere reiteration. As far as the "return" aspect is concerned, in *diachrony* several elements can be summoned. First, the *pleasure principle* is subjected to a kind of reading that dissects it: as expected, Laplanche slips in the knife to show that this principle is split into two opposite tendencies: a tendency on the side of satisfaction related to the "constancy principle" (and hence to the ego as organization, in its metaphorical deriva-

45 *L&D*, p. 85.
46 See, in particular, the debate with André Green in *La pulsion de mort*, Green et al., Paris: PUF, 1986.

tion); and a tendency on the side of *jouissance* related to the *principle of neuronal inertia*.[47] This tendency to zero-point energy is perfectly aligned with the death drive viewed from an economic perspective. But Laplanche is supported by something else when he uncovers the theoretical constraint that leads Freud to rely on the death drive to balance his entire theoretical edifice. An excerpt from "Minutes of the Vienna Psychoanalytic Society" recounts the discussions of this small circle led by Freud, on April 20 and 27, 1910. On the basis of this very short text, Laplanche establishes that the "life drive" is already featured in the thought of Freud and his circle long before the turning point of the 1920s. He also shows that the life drive is on the side of ego drives and that, far from coinciding with sexuality, it stands in direct opposition to it. "In the first theory of the drives," Laplanche concludes, "sexuality, as a disruptive force, is what signals the place of the forthcoming 'death drive'."[48]

In *synchrony*, the concept of the death drive is necessitated by the merging of sexuality as a disruptive force with sexuality as linked to the ego (to narcissism) under the aegis of Eros. The excessive "civility" of the sexual—Eros had to be counterbalanced, especially since Freud remained faithful to the basic economic principle of psychoanalysis in its most absolute form: the tendency to discharge or to return to zero, the principle of neuronal inertia. For these reasons, Laplanche prefers to speak of the *sexual life drives* and the *sexual death drives* and, for the sake of accuracy, to specify their opposition on the basis of their different regimes: binding for the sexual life drives, unbinding for the sexual death drives.[49]

This complex issue well illustrates the kind of clarifications

---

47 The "principle of neuronal inertia" was first articulated by Freud in the *Project for a Scientific Psychology*: "This is the principle of neuronal inertia: that neurones tend to divest themselves of Q" (*SE* I, 296). Laplanche refers to this principle as *"principe du zéro."*

48 "Pulsion de vie—1910," in *La révolution copernicienne inachevée*, pp. 135–136.

49 "La pulsion de mort dans la théorie sexuelle," in *La révolution copernicienne inachevée*, pp. 273–286. See also *NF*, pp. 139–147.

and in-depth elaborations characteristic of Laplanche's contributions to fundamental questions in psychoanalysis. The diffraction of concepts, his "hacking them with a pickax," as he sometimes puts it, are operations fully consistent with the analytic project as implemented in the analytic treatment itself. But this "lytic" work does not consist, at the outset, in choosing between the various conceptual lines, whether they be parallel, divergent, or in full-fledged opposition. The point of this radical unfurling of Freud's text, akin to the analyst's listening with evenly suspended attention during the analytic session, consists mainly in watching the concepts work before our eyes and, after methodically breaking them apart, watching them recohere in a new organization. But it goes further: the point is to work "underground" in order to consolidate and buttress the parts of the psychoanalytic edifice that require it. Through a kind of *retrogression* within the theory itself, it is no longer the birth of sexuality as a phenomenon that the concept of leaning-on serves to describe (as was mainly the case in *Life and Death in Psychoanalysis,* as we have seen). It now accounts for the aim of the analytic work applied to Freud's theory: to identify the weak parts in its foundations and, following a stringent critique, to provide new foundations.

Parenthesis: Psychoanalysis in the University

After *Life and Death,* Laplanche embarked on a series of conceptual research projects. The results of this research, initially presented as lectures, were then published in five volumes under the general title of *Problématiques*: *L'Angoisse, Castration, Symbolisations, La Sublimation, L'Inconscient et le* ça (*The Unconscious and the Id*), and *Le baquet–Transcendance du transfert.*[50] As this research project involved

---

50 Translator's note: There are now seven volumes in all. *Problématiques IV* and *VII* have been translated into English: *Problématiques IV* as "The Unconscious and the Id," Trans. Luke Thurston with Lindsay Watson, London: Rebus Press, 1999; *Problématiques VII* as "The Temptation of Biology: Freud's Theories of Sexuality," Trans. Donald Nicholson-Smith. New York: Unconscious in Translation, 2015.

teaching, it affords me the opportunity to address another area in which Laplanche made outstanding contributions: the presence of psychoanalysis in the university.

Starting in 1962, Laplanche held public seminars at the Ecole Normale and the Sorbonne. After 1969, his teaching was done in the Department of Clinical Human Sciences at the University of Paris VII. In 1980, a doctoral program in psychoanalysis was established there. All this might seem rather banal these days; there are now several university programs in psychoanalytic studies, not only in France but also in the Anglo-American world. I will discuss how such programs can easily lead to misunderstandings, but let us begin by specifying what the teaching of psychoanalysis in the university aims to achieve so far as Laplanche is concerned.

The academic teaching of psychoanalysis consists, first and foremost, in developing psychoanalysis as a tool, as a field of study, and as a fully recognized discipline alongside the other academic disciplines. The point is to inscribe and maintain psychoanalysis within the scientific community, as the title of one of Laplanche's texts on the subject makes clear.[51] At the same time, however, psychoanalysis must also be acknowledged as a distinct science among all the others—a science that relates to the other sciences in a way different from how they relate to one another. Psychoanalysis as a discipline must then be able to arrive at the results of its own method as universalizable statements, as it were. Laplanche writes: "To speak *of Psychoanalysis* implies . . . that our discipline can be set forth as statements that are transmissible, testable, arguable, even 'falsifiable' (as they put it in certain epistemological circles); the point, in short, is that one cannot say any old thing about Psychoanalysis."[52] To claim a legitimate place among scientific disciplines, psychoanalysis must also delineate its own specific object.

---

51 J. Laplanche, "La psychanalyse dans la communauté scientifique," *Cliniques méditerranéennes* 45/46, 1995, pp. 33–42.
52 *P5*, p. 138.

In his writings, specifically in the introduction to *New Foundations* and in *Problématiques V*, Laplanche discusses what he calls "the sites of the psychoanalytic experience."[53] In addition to treatment, which he regards as the foundational site, Laplanche distinguishes three others: extramural psychoanalysis (outside the walls of the analytic session), psychoanalytic theory, and the history of psychoanalysis. Laplanche prefers the term "extramural psychoanalysis" or, alternatively, "exported" or "transposed" psychoanalysis to "applied psychoanalysis," a term that assigns this practice a lesser place and suggests a sort of psychoanalytic engineering, the mere "superimposition" on some object of an abstract theory and method from another domain. "Extramural" in no way implies that extramural psychoanalysis applies to everything and anything: it refers specifically to the area of cultural phenomena, the area where psychoanalysis may rightfully set out its interpretive, theoretical, and even speculative acts, all the more so as psychoanalysis itself has entered the cultural sphere and constitutes a broad cultural movement, a fact that has a feedback effect on what psychoanalysis might have to say about culture. Modern humanity is not only studied by but also culturally marked by psychoanalysis.[54]

Laplanche draws together these four sites of the analytic experience under the category of *the theoretic* (*le théorétique*). The term is meant to include both theory and clinical work and to prevent a split between the two that would confine clinical psychoanalysis to the limits of a "practice" while limiting theory to sheer speculation almost devoid of serious consequences. The theoretic stems from the fact that "even what is known as clinical psychoanalysis is in fact a certain *consideration* (*theorein*) of—or reflection on—its object, for there can be no clinical psychoanalysis in a purely empirical sense."[55]

---

53 Translator's note: As mentioned earlier, the French word *expérience* means both "experience" and "experiment."
54 *NF*, p. 12-13. Also see *P5*, pp. 146–148.
55 *NF*, p. 15.

As I have suggested, however, the idea of a university program in psychoanalysis can occasion questions and misunderstandings, starting with one that Laplanche is quick to address: does this university education aim at training analysts? Laplanche's position on the subject has always been clear. To those concerned with the possible implementation of a "vocational training" program at the university, Laplanche replies that such a goal would be at odds with his views of psychoanalysis itself and of the training of analysts. These views are the direct outcome of his theoretical positions as we have seen them develop. To Laplanche, delineating the specific field of psychoanalysis, deriving it from fields centered on self-interest or the adaptational sphere, points to the radical extraterritoriality of psychoanalytic practice in relation to institutions. He invokes the basic Freudian precept—the corollary of the fundamental rule in psychoanalysis—which consists in the *suspension of purposive ideas*. Without this precept, analysis would promptly fall back on the adaptational aims upheld by the institutions in question, even if such aims pertain to the training of analysts. Laplanche not only opposes the training of analysts in the university; he is a fierce opponent also of what is called a "training" psychoanalysis, the kind of analysis that even today, in many psychoanalytic institutes throughout the world, is required of analytic candidates. How can the commitment to genuine analytic work be compatible with in any way determining its outcome, in this instance the training of an analyst? Yet, Laplanche does not object to training analyses in the name of a "therapeutic" ideal. The therapeutic aim is but another "purposive idea" that must itself be suspended, however praiseworthy it might be. No purposive idea of any kind should interfere as a distraction or impediment: the process of reinstatement implemented in and through the analysis must comprise *every* ego formation. This includes therapeutic aims, which themselves must be analyzed. "It is claimed," Laplanche writes, "that the desire to become an analyst is 'analyzable' as any other desire might be. But it is a sham analysis as soon as the institute is, as it were, waiting at the door of the consulting room, just like a mother in the waiting room, waiting for her child who is *analyzed on her orders* so that he or she may become 'good'."[56]

Later in his work, Laplanche's reflection on psychoanalysis in the university led to perhaps even more radical developments that raise the issue of the scientific status of psychoanalytic theory. Unsurprisingly, Laplanche discerns two levels here: on the one hand, *metapsychological theory*, which in his view has scientific status; on the other, the "theories" that psychoanalysis encounters in people's minds (e.g., infantile sexual theories). I mentioned something more radical about Laplanche's development: what he denounces here is the general tendency not to distinguish between these two theoretical levels. "There is a confusion that is often present," he notes, "between 'theories' as tools of self-interpretation created by a human being, and psychoanalytic theories which, among other things, must certainly account for the function of spontaneous or ideological 'theories'."[57] An example is the theory of castration, a theory that Laplanche ascribes to "Hans and Sigmund" in the sense that, through a plethora of fantasies, Little Hans conveyed the content of this "complex," which should not be confused with a theoretical statement of psychoanalysis. It is, indeed, a spontaneous "theory" of Little Hans—and of many others—a "theory" whose function psychoanalysis is called upon to determine. For example, in this case, the function would be to master the primal anxiety arising from the attack of sexual excitation, a function Freud did not miss.

The confusion is blatant when the "theory" of castration is raised to the level of psychoanalytic theory, or even seen in terms of a goal of analysis, as when it is claimed that the end of analysis consists in one's ability to "assume castration." Laplanche points to the harmful consequence of such a confusion between theory and "theo-

---

56 J. Laplanche, "La didactique: une psychanalyse 'sur commande'," *Trans* 3, Autumn 1993, p. 79.
57 J. Laplanche, "La psychanalyse dans la communauté scientifique," *op. cit.*, p. 38.

ries": "theories" morph into ideologies inadvertently transmitted in the context of the analysis. Castration is thus "given a metaphysical dimension . . . , a rather hasty synonym of 'finitude'. But it remains just as fundamentally ideological, not more or less respectable than other ideological terms that were exposed as such in the past, like 'free enterprise' or the 'American way of life'."[58] The important point as far as the scientific status of psychoanalysis is concerned is that such ideologized "theories" are more likely to substantiate critiques of psychoanalysis (like that of Karl Popper) as "nonrefutable." Metapsychology, conversely, the true theoretical plane of psychoanalysis is, like every theory, "a construction that aims to be as simple, as elegant, and as rigorous as possible in the way that it accounts for facts. It is therefore the object of a *critique* as regards its simplicity, its elegance and its relevance; the object of *refutation* as regards its internal coherence; and, finally, the object of *falsification*, i.e. of a possible confrontation of its findings with its facts."[59]

Retracing the Primal

New Foundations for Psychoanalysis is a pivotal text in Laplanche's body of work. On reflection, it is the perfect illustration of its subject matter. "Let us be wary of the term 'new'," Laplanche states in the opening pages, and he immediately quotes Freud, for whom every step forward is always only half as big as it looks at first. We can certainly endorse this adage, having seen how Laplanche launched a critique of the theory of leaning-on in *Life and Death*— however pivotal this theory might be to the book—thus paving the way for the general theory of seduction that would emerge clearly as early as 1975, in the context of Laplanche's seminar on sublima-

---

58 *Op. cit.*, pp. 38–39.
59 *Op. cit.*, p. 36.

tion (*Problématiques III*).[60] Is *New Foundations* simply a return? Let us reverse Freud's adage and suggest that returns are never as repetitive as one might think, at least when they are inscribed in the kind of spiral elaboration characteristic of Laplanche, each turn of the spiral being more than a summary of research, but rather itself a re-foundation, a reinstatement of the primal within psychoanalysis.

Let me be more specific. Published in 1987, as the outcome of a long research project documented, in part, by the five volumes of the *Problématiques* series, *New Foundations for Psychoanalysis* explicitly aspires to revisit the theory of seduction, from the point at which Freud reportedly abandoned it. Predictably, for Laplanche, revisiting the theory of seduction does not imply taking it up "as is," but rather subjecting it to some form of work: in *New Foundations*, the kind of work in question is a process of reinstatement. Its aim is to *retrace* origins, in the sense both of recapturing and of reinscribing. The composition of the book mirrors the evolution it examines; the first part is titled "Catharsis," thus seeming to start out from the immediate historical precedents to Freud's theory of seduction—namely, Breuer's cathartic method. The process of retracing the primal thus inscribes within the book itself a return to historical origins. But as I was suggesting, returns are less repetitive than one might think: Laplanche does not return to the cathartic theory per se; instead he *effects* a true catharsis regarding the many developments that, in a variety of psychoanalytic traditions since Freud, have built upon "the famous cataclysm brought about by the so-called abandoning of the seduction theory."[61] For in Laplanche's view this cataclysm has not been sufficiently worked through.

---

60 *P3*, pp. 50–69.
61 *NF*, p. 15.

From Forms of the Primal to
Morphisms in the Unconscious

In the catharsis section, Laplanche makes a few necessary adjustments, clearing out the clutter in order to refind the landmarks and boundaries of the psychoanalytic field. Such a systematic critique aims at delineating a specific psychoanalytic domain on the basis of "neighboring fields . . . because [the psychoanalytic field] stands out against them, because it can be contrasted with them. But, I repeat, the fact that it stands out means that the background does not remain unchanged. Its emergence has a *foundational* import, just as the gesture which creates the psychoanalytic situation has a foundational import, a re-foundational import."[62] Laplanche starts with an examination of the forms in which the primal traditionally appears in psychoanalysis. He distinguishes four forms: biological, phylogenetic, mechanical, and linguistic, and he demonstrates how none of these can be said to be at the origin of the psychoanalytic domain.

Biology: while it goes without saying that "we are living beings before we become human beings or 'cultural' beings,"[63] the issue of whether the biological sphere presides over the genesis of the human psyche remains unsettled. Laplanche lists all the objections to the notion of biological ascendancy, including the *false biology* resorted to by Freud when he proposes a biological foundation. "The ego is likened to a substance that lives inside the individual," Laplanche writes, "but it is a rudimentary living substance or even a false image of a living substance; it is something which remains constant in the face of something that metaphorically transforms internal attacks (those that come from the drives) into external attacks."[64] "Biomorphism" thus consists in a representation, a metaphorization, of the biological order, *in the image of* the biological but not biological in itself.

---

62 *NF*, pp. 53–54 (translation modified).
63 *NF*, p. 21.
64 *NF*, p. 22.

Equally problematic is the *phylogenetic* form, which arises principally in terms of *primal fantasies* that Freud thought were genetically transmitted. To Laplanche, the idea of biologically inscribed mnemonic scenarios is objectionable insofar as it embeds a confusion between *memory* (which is always linked with representations) and *behavioral schemas* (which can indeed be inherited). Nevertheless, Laplanche does not deny that Freud, thanks to his posit of primal fantasies, discovered something prototypical that at once surpasses and informs individual lived experience. The discovery in question, however, once again consists in a kind of rediscovery: this is illustrated by the fantasy of castration insofar as it features one of the "theories" I have discussed: an infantile sexual theory. Far from being the human equivalent of instinct in animals, as Freud claimed, the "primal fantasy" of castration "is primarily an *answer* and not a drive-related questioning. It is an answer to one of the many agonizing questions young children ask: What is the origin of the difference between the sexes?"[65] Therefore, because they are topographically "secondary" as instances of self-theorization on the part of the human child, fantasies of this kind are not present at the outset. They presuppose that their "transmission" should take place as a "secondary logical pattern which is inherent in verbal communication."[66]

Freud's use of mechanical models stems from the influence of physicalism professed by a group of scientists including Ernst Brücke, Freud's mentor in biology. To Laplanche, the recourse to mechanics to account for the foundational state of the biological organism is indefensible, yet he also notes that such sham physics must nonetheless correspond to something: not anything foundational, however, but to something deeply buried, "in the third person," "in the form of the id,"[67]

As one might anticipate, the *linguistic* form of the primal

---

65 *NF*, p. 36 (translation modified).
66 *NF*, p. 37.
67 See "The Question of the Id," in *P4*.

gives Laplanche a prime opportunity to take up a position in relation to Lacan's famous mantra: "the unconscious is structured like a language." To Laplanche, positing verbal language in the deepest stratum is thoroughly anti-Freudian insofar as, in Freud's view, verbal language is secondary in every sense of the word. It is secondary historically, topographically (language is characteristic of the ego and the preconscious), and economically (language is ruled by modes of associations and circulation that are identified as secondary process). Laplanche, however, welcomes the notion of the signifier, which he inscribes within a semiological framework rather than a purely linguistic one and which, he contends, is in keeping with Saussure's ambition. Yet he rejects the idealism of upholding the primacy of the signifier. From Lacan he retains the basic distinction between "signifier *of*" and "signifier *to*," a distinction he puts to use in asserting that "a signifier can signify *to* someone without the person addressed knowing what is being signified."[68]

The critique of recourse to false biology, false anthropology, false physics, and false linguistics does not exclude the fact that such recourses are nevertheless *representative* of some aspect of the psychoanalytic object. This offers a clear illustration of Laplanche's method of reading: the point is not to choose for or against one side of what, in any case, seems like a false dichotomy but to retrace the origins of the dichotomy and map it out in a different way. In the psyche, there is something *like* a biological form, *like* an anthropological form, etc. For Laplanche, the unconscious is "like a non–structured language."

Approaching the Primal

If the field of psychoanalysis is not based on exogenous premises but integrates those external domains only as representational

---

68 *NF*, p. 44 (translation modified).

morphisms, then what *is* it founded on? A first answer to this question is that it is founded on a self-foundational situation, a situation that arises from the act of delineation itself, from the mapping-out of a specific space: it is the enclosure of the analytic session, delineating the "tub" (*baquet*) of the treatment, which Laplanche posits as homologous to Freud's view of the psychic apparatus as revealed by the study of dreams.[69] The fact of being founded on a unique practice defines a field that is itself specific, thus carrying out a process of exclusion that *Life and Death in Psychoanalysis* has made familiar to us: namely, exclusion of the adaptational domain—also referred to as the realm of self-interest and as the realm of self-preservation. This process of exclusion is deliberate and methodologically justified because it is based on the border marked out by the process of leaning-on. Its logical implication is that psychoanalysis cannot claim the entire psychological field as its own. Consequently, what is required in order to approach the primal, and to locate the field of psychoanalysis specifically attached to it, is a rigorous critique of what Laplanche refers to as *panpsychoanalyticism*.

The closure of the analytic "tub" is quite relative, as Laplanche specifies, inasmuch as the latter does not enclose the situation within some absolute *hic et nunc* but remains instead open to the past—open, among other things, to the historical dimension. The history in question, however, is not history in general; psychoanalysts have not dispensed with the burden of biology or linguistics to become historians. The history under discussion is precisely the history of the emergence of man as the object of psychoanalysis, which differs from human beings in general: at stake is the self-theorizing, self-symbolizing being, this "human object insofar as it formulates its own experience and gives it a form."[70] As suggested earlier, such history therefore stands out, or is retraced, against the backdrop of a broader history that necessarily consists in the history of individual develop-

---

69 See "Le baquet," in *Problématiques 5*.
70 *NF*, p. 10 (translation modified).

ment. In keeping with what was previously established regarding neighboring disciplines, such a development is to be understood not as a "natural" pathway to the unconscious (via some process of emergence) but rather as a sequence in which the unconscious, as specified by the sexual, *occurs, intervenes, intrudes.* The history under consideration—and the same could be held true of an archaeology[71]—is precisely what yields an understanding of the conditions underlying the advent of the unconscious. The historical or archaeological terrain where the unconscious emerges and becomes inscribed as an event is what Laplanche refers to as *primal (originaire).*

"The primal is something which transcends time but which is also bound up with time."[72] This comment is a warning against the facile recourse to some mythical dimension in order to characterize the time of the origins, one that often resurfaces when psychoanalysts seek to circumvent the developmental sphere. The primal according to Laplanche precisely avoids these two shortcomings: the risk of confusing the psychoanalytic and the developmental spheres and the risk of referring back to a so-called mythical time. Such a critique of the reliance on the mythical in psychoanalysis goes back to 1964, when, in "Primal Fantasy, Fantasies of Origins, Origins of Fantasy," Laplanche and Pontalis denounced the senselessness of resorting to myth in order to compensate for an exceedingly elusive chronology. "The myth (or the fantasy) of the intrusion of the fantasy (or myth) into the subject must itself occur at some point in the life of the little human, a point at which as a function of his biological development we can already read the too much and the too little, the too soon (birth) and the too late (puberty)."[73] In *New Foundations,* Laplanche

71 Due to limited space, I cannot provide an account of Laplanche's important ideas on the relation between psychoanalysis and the historical and archaeological models. Cf. "La psychanalyse: histoire ou archeology," *RCI,* pp. 185–211, and "Interpretation: Between Determinism and Hermeneutics," *Essays on Otherness,* pp. 138–165.
72 *NF,* p. 59.
73 J. Laplanche & J.-B. Pontalis, "Primal Fantasy, Fantasies of Origins, Origins of Fantasy" in this volume p. 86.

also points out that, far from accounting for the origin, the recourse to myth (the power of self-mythification or self-theorization) is exactly what psychoanalysis is called upon to explain.

But if the primal is not subsumed in the mythic, it cannot be added to the developmental either. This has been a common confusion in psychoanalysis. Though critical of it, Laplanche also excuses it in these terms: "It is because the whole *thrust of human life* consists in re-inhabiting—or if you prefer reinvesting—all of psychic life with sexual motivations that are largely unconscious."[74] The basic epistemological problem that comes with tackling the pre- or extra-analytic sphere has already been emphasized. It partly accounts for *pansexualism* (the tendency to consider everything as sexual) and pan-psychoanalyticism (or, as it were, an imperialistic tendency that posits psychoanalysis as the whole of psychology). As a consequence of the fact that the sexual is called upon to buttress self-preservation, which is deficient in humans, pansexualism is a tendency of human reality before being a theoretical aberration in need of correction.

Panpsychoanalyticism is but a debased version of this pan-sexualism, stemming from the fact that the sexual—which subsumes the vital order—loses its luster, being folded into the vital order itself, thus blurring the border between psychoanalysis and psychology. Among the examples of this confusion, Laplanche stresses the confusion between the object of the sexual wish (*Wunsch*) and the object of need and perception, or between objectality (refinding a sexual object following the path traced by the *Wunsch*) and objectivity (delineating and positing as independent a motor-perceptive object). As another example, he also mentions the shift from the kind of wish fulfillment referred to as "hallucinatory" to the insertion of an allegedly hallucinatory stage as a step toward accessing external reality. Yet another example is the confusion between sexual narcissism and the absence of any targeted real object (or the nondifferentiation between

---

74 *NF*, p. 60 (translation modified).

subject and object, or, alternatively, symbiosis). "This reductionism," Laplanche remarks, "results in more than conceptual confusion; phases and stages of development are superimposed. The whole of development is being described in terms which Freud applies specifically to the emergence of sexuality. But if Freudian psychoanalysis gains a hold on development, it is completely emptied out of its substance because development as a whole is desexualized."[75]

Reconfiguration of the specific field of psychoanalysis requires that these confusions be cleared up. This restores a legitimate place for developmental psychology and infant observation (including psychoanalytic observation), provided one bears in mind that, while any form of observation is by definition indirect—no observation can dispense with hypotheses for which direct verification is impossible—psychoanalytic observation is doubly indirect: (1) in the way any attempt to acquire knowledge might be; (2) because its very object is "indirect." This pertains to the distinctive temporality of psychoanalysis, a temporality featuring *après-coup* and functioning according to two phases, neither of which is identifiable separately as a result of always being suspended between a "too soon" and a "too late."

Toward a General Theory of Seduction

Having clarified the conceptual landscape of the primal, we still need to account for the situation the primal encapsulates. Before tackling this issue, a methodological note is in order: because the task consists in describing the conditions in which the unconscious—the sexual unconscious—comes into being, we must reject the possibility that this sexuality is already be present on the "terrain" where it emerges. In passing, let us stress Laplanche's methodological rigor when, for the purposes of proof, he does not presume that what is

---

75 *NF*, p. 68 (translation modified).

found at the end was present at the outset. While the primal situation brings together a child and an adult, we must reject the notion that the child's sexuality is "already there." We must also reject the notion that the adult purely and simply "transmits" his or her unconscious sexuality to the child; otherwise, what we get is a process of infinite regress from sexuality to sexuality or from one unconscious to the other, which in the end would explain nothing. This is an important clarification, as many readers of Laplanche misunderstand this point: it is clear that the adult in the primal situation *is* endowed with an unconscious in the full sense of the term, but there is no way that this unconscious can be transmitted directly. The hiatus, the disparity, between the adult and the child creates a space in which an active process of metabolization must be carried out by the child, a process whose partial failure accounts for that "residue" called the unconscious.

Laplanche describes the child in the primal situation as a *biopsychical being*; let us remember that the psychic is not wholly within the sphere of the sexual unconscious, but that there is also the mental belonging to self-preservation. Let us also remember that the theory of leaning-on does not describe the body/soul relation but rather that it delineates the relation between self-preservation and sexuality. Such a being is open to the world (see the critique of a presupposed anobjectal state), equipped with physiological and psychophysiological (or instinctual) self-regulatory mechanisms but is essentially incapable of helping itself (*Hilflösigkeit*), as much because of organic immaturity as of its complete unawareness of danger.

The adult in the primal situation is essentially characterized by the dimension of the unconscious, of an unconscious "at the most visible level." The adult in question cannot account for *all* of her actions because, for example, the adult will inevitably have parapraxes (slips of the tongue and the like). In other words, what characterizes this adult is that she transmits much more than she is conscious of transmitting. What's more, this adult is *deviant* with regard to any norms concerning sexuality (not as a case of individual perversion but on account of the essential deviance of human sexuality) and with regard to herself, due to the very fact of having an unconscious (*inconscienci-alité*, the unconscious in the descriptive sense); deviant also because a child always dwells in the adult, so that relating to a child inevitably summons the infantile within. "The primal relationship is therefore established on a twofold register: we have both a vital, open and reciprocal relationship, which can truly be said to be interactive, and a relationship that involves sexuality but is no longer interactive in the same way because the two partners are not equal."[76]

In *retracing* primal seduction, Laplanche implements a procedure that relies on the analytic rules we are used to seeing him apply. The point is to identify with the utmost precision both the effects of the "cataclysm" entailed by Freud's abandonment of the seduction theory, and the fate of the various components of that theory. The theory abandoned by Freud is the *special theory of seduction*,[77] insofar as its interest in seduction was strictly tied to psychopathology: the theory was concerned with the pathology of the victim (it aimed to account for the etiology of hysteria), with the pathology of the seducer (the essentially perverse adult/father), and also with the mechanisms involved (repression was seen by Freud as a pathological defense while the unconscious itself made up a pathological domain to be conquered by the analysis). Such a restriction to pathology was thus highly contingent on factuality: the identification of events, of actual facts. Yet in practice such factuality turned out to be undercut by the fact that it led back from one scene of seduction to another earlier one, always giving Freud the hope that he would finally be led back to the "real" scene—and always encountering disappointment. These two factors (factuality and the restriction to pathology) contributed to the

---

76 *NF*, p. 103 (translation modified).

77 Translator's note: The French phrase is *théorie restreinte,* suggesting a parallel with Einstein's two theories of relativity: special relativity (*relativité restreinte*) and general relativity (*relativité générale*). To retain the reference to Einstein, *théorie restreinte* will be translated as "special theory" and *théorie générale* as "general theory."

failure of this theory and to Freud's ultimate rejection of it.

Even though he has no desire to salvage the theory in its original form, Laplanche is, as usual, able to identify the key elements that gave it strength. In Laplanche's view, this strength stems from the tight weaving between the theory and the facts of the analytic experience, which allowed Freud—as read by Laplanche—to distinguish three essential elements or aspects: (1) the temporal aspect: this pertains to the temporality of *après-coup,* as discussed with regard to the "Emma" case; (2) the topographical aspect: an aspect linked to *après-coup* that consists in seeing the assault as an internal one and therefore as pertaining to the topographical differentiation of the apparatus of the soul; (3) the linguistic-translational aspect: this aspect involves the successive transcriptions of memory traces as described by Freud in a letter to Fliess, the famous "Letter 52."[78] Between these transcriptions, the language specific to one stage would undergo a kind of translation into the language of the next stage, a translation process that would occasionally fail; according to Freud, such *failures of translation* coincide with repression. Freud's abandonment of the theory as a unified whole launched these three elements on different paths: while *après-coup* survived, if only barely, until Lacan gave it a second wind, the linguistic-translational aspect was completely eradicated by Freud. It was rediscovered by Ferenczi, independently, in a text that features, according to Laplanche, "a kind of preface to the general theory of seduction."[79] The topographical aspect endured, though it underwent a complete reversal: in the complex temporal sequence of *après-coup,* the internal assault, which Freud continued to uphold, was no longer ascribed to traumatic reminiscence; rather, it was attributed to the drive considered as originating in the biological sphere.

---

78 See *SE* I.
79 The text in question is "Confusion of the Tongues between the Adults and the Child" , by S. Ferenczi, German original in *Internationale Zeitschrift fur Psychoanalyse* (1933) 19: 5-10; English translation in *International Journal of Psychoanalysis* (1949) 30:225–230.

Regarding factuality, however, Laplanche underlines a progression in Freud's reflection, insofar as the perverse father featured in the first theory of seduction (in what Laplanche refers to as *infantile seduction*) is replaced by the mother, who in the course of the most normal nursery care subjects the child to a process of involuntary seduction (*early seduction* in Laplanche's classification). This bears witness to the fact that seduction has not been completely abandoned after all and that, what's more, it has even been freed from the strict limits of psychopathology and thus reinscribed in the universal mother-child relationship: involuntary seduction, but inexorable seduction all the same. Yet Freud is still committed to factuality, as he attributes the awakening of the child's genital organs to the effects of bodily care, though he neglects the presence and power of the unconscious of the other person—of the mother—and consequently fails to locate seduction in a sufficiently broad theoretical context. Seduction is still a fact and, in spite of everything, remains in the realm of contingent events which Freud refers to as the "accidental."

General Seduction and Psychic Decentering

Laplanche's work essentially consists in releasing seduction from this relation to events, however inescapable they may be, in order to formulate a *theory* of seduction. He sets out to do so through a process of theoretical questioning, starting with a reexamination of the active/passive dichotomy.

From a behavioral perspective, notes Laplanche, positing an unequal distribution of activity and passivity between the child and the adult is erroneous. The observation of infants provides ample evidence that the human child, despite the relative deficiency of its instinctual schemata, is far from passive in relating to the mother. Thus, passivity is not located on the side of the vital order. When seduction is mentioned, however, it means there is a seducer and a seduced, which reintroduces the notion of passivity; this is true in Freud's texts, despite his occasional confusion on the issue. Hence the need to reconsider the question of passivity. To do so, Laplanche draws on philosophical thought, especially that of Spinoza, for whom the soul is active when it has "adequate ideas" and passive when its ideas are "inadequate". This is not a behavioral form of passivity but a basic asymmetry operating on another level: the gap between adult and child, an imbalance stemming from an "excess of message" arising from the adult. This is the meaning Laplanche gives to Ferenczi's contribution which he inscribes in his development of the general theory of seduction. Indeed, Ferenczi speaks of the confrontation between two worlds, the adult's and the child's, two worlds that do not share the same language. Laplanche retains this idea, not in terms of *languages* as Ferenczi does, but in his assertion that, in the eyes of the child, what characterizes the adult's world are messages that "ask the child questions he cannot yet understand but to which he must attribute meaning and give a response."[80] The languages we find at this juncture are not the decisive factor. Laplanche is resolutely at odds with the Lacanian project on this point. The point Laplanche makes is that the child enters language without a teacher because the child inhabits language. The polysemy of language invoked by Lacan is not at stake either. The essential passivity of the child does not pertain to language as a general, transindividual structure; it operates instead at the level of the *meaning* of the messages, a meaning that remains enigmatic to the child, all the more so as it is enigmatic for the adult who transmits the messages. To Laplanche, the adult's "language of passion," as Ferenczi calls it, "is traumatic only insofar as it conveys a meaning that is unknown to itself, that is to say insofar as it manifests the presence of the parental unconscious."[81] As I have emphasized, Laplanche does not imply that there is a transmission of the adult's unconscious into the child's unconscious. The presence of

---

80 *NF*, pp. 124–125 (translation modified).
81 *NF*, p. 125 (translation modified).

the adult's unconscious is revealed precisely by the enigmatic nature of the message: the unconscious is featured in the adult message in a strictly concealed form, following the structure of neurotic symptoms. The child must implement his own procedures to metabolize the enigmatic message arising from the other, and what such procedures yield is topographical differentiation.

The heart of the matter is in sight: "I am then using the term *primal seduction* to describe a fundamental situation in which an adult proffers to a child verbal, non-verbal and even behavioral signifiers which are pregnant with unconscious sexual significations."[82] Laplanche at first uses the term "enigmatic signifier" to refer to that which *signifies to* the child, that which addresses the child. Later he revisits this formulation, preferring the term "enigmatic message" and finally settling on "compromised message." *Message* rather than *signifier* because the latter always refers to an isolated linguistic unit and there is no need to "translate a signifier." We shall soon see the importance of translation in this process. *Compromised* rather than *enigmatic* so as to prevent any possible misunderstanding regarding the effective element in the message. To be seductive, the kind of enigma discussed by Laplanche must be an enigma for the transmitter as well. This can be true only to the extent that the enigma in question is acted on by the transmitter's unconscious. It is thus less ambiguous to refer to a "compromised message" in the sense of "contamination" by the adult's unconscious.

The *category of the message* is, in Laplanche's view, a way to solve the endless dilemma between psychological reality and material reality. Let us not forget that Freud posited the concept of psychic reality without really managing to theorize it; he uses the term "to designate whatever in the subject's psyche presents a consistency and resistance comparable to those displayed by material reality."[83] To Laplanche,

---

82 *NF*, p. 126.
83 J. Laplanche & J.-B. Pontalis, *The Language of Psycho-analysis*, op. cit., p. 363.

this psychic reality is akin to what he calls "the reality of the message," a reality whose materiality is the signifier and that dwells not so much adjacent to the two other orders of reality but perpendicular to them. One need not choose, then, between psychic reality (the fact is that even the most nonsensical idea is a psychological event that can possibly be identified neurophysiologically) and material reality. Rather, one must take into account the specific reality that arises in human relations as a result of the enigmatic message, a message that affects the recipient because it is itself affected (or contaminated) by the transmitter's unconscious. The reality of the message is at bottom the reality of whatever always *parasitizes* intersubjective communication. However clear the communication may be, the recipient is left with the question "What does he, the emitter, want from me?" denoting the nonmetabolized residue of communication. This residue imposes a *demand for work* on the psychic apparatus of the recipient, a demand that establishes its role, a role that Laplanche identifies as the *source-object of the drive*[84] (see below).

Hierarchy of the Levels of Seduction

The theory of primal seduction has numerous implications. I will underline a few but first give this clarification: primal seduction does not replace early seduction or infantile seduction; it does not invalidate their importance but instead provides them a foundation. It is in this sense of foundation that we can speak of a hierarchy, not in the sense of a temporal sequence involving the three levels. Primal seduction is not an initial stage of seduction to be followed by infantile or early seduction as a second stage. Endowed with its own effectiveness, primal seduction also allows us to understand the

---

84 See "The Drive and Its Source-Object: Its Fate in the Transference," in *Essays on Otherness*, pp. 120–135.

other two, to *theorize* them beyond their factuality, beyond their episodic, contingent, "accidental" nature. "Primal seduction," Laplanche writes, "is the ultimate essence of the other two stages, insofar as it alone introduces the 'activity–passivity' asymmetry. 'Maternal' care or 'paternal' aggression are seductive only because they are not transparent but opaque, because they carry enigmas."[85] Early seduction, which is related to maternal care, can therefore be freed from the impasses that follow from Freud's description which centers on awakening of genital sensations. Freud's account leaves us with the problem of how to ascertain the nature of what is sexual when other erotogenic zones are involved, or when the erotogenicity of the entire body is at stake.[86] The impasse is overcome when, in the context of primal seduction, "one remembers that such zones, such sites of transit and exchanges are, first and foremost, the focal points of maternal care, care related to hygiene which solicitude motivates consciously but in which unconscious wishful fantasies are fully active."[87]

Translation, Its Failure, and the Institution of the Unconscious

The fundamental asymmetry between the adult and the child in terms of messages forces the task of mastering and symbolizing on the child, a task which one could call *translation*. It is a process of translation which, due to the fundamental asymmetry, can never be complete and must therefore always leave untranslated residues. These untranslated residues, forever remaining "to be translated," repeatedly present the child with a demand for the work of symbolization. That Laplanche makes these residues the *source-objects of the*

---

85 *NF*, p. 128 (translation modified).
86 This problem is closely related to the issue of leaning-on, which Laplanche discusses at length in *FBS*, pp. 36–43 especially.
87 *NF*, p. 128 (translation modified).

drive is hardly surprising as soon as one realizes, in hindsight, that this account is exactly in keeping with Freud's description of the drive: that which imposes a demand for work on the psychic apparatus. But by locating the sources of the drive in the unmastered, untranslated residues of the other's message, as opposed to some simple metonymical derivation of adaptational somatic functions, Laplanche is dramatically distancing himself from the theory of leaning-on. This does not imply that the body is excluded from this model; it is only to say that the compromised message of the other designates the bodily zones where the source-objects are implanted. *Primal repression*, the process that establishes the topographical partition between unconscious and preconscious-conscious, stems from the necessity to counter-invest these residues which, in their untranslated state, continue to be internal sources of excitation. The messages, with their enigmatic character, have been metabolized into two parts by the translation process: one part has been translated into a preconscious-conscious memory; another part has fallen out of the translation spectrum and thus become a source-object of the drive.

Let us point out, in passing, that the term *source-object* has more than one resonance: to begin with, it inscribes the relation between the source and the object of the drive in a kind of loop—or spiral, in keeping with Laplanche's vocabulary—whereas Freud envisions this relation in linear terms. Just as Hölderlin's river flows in the direction of its source,[88] the drive, as Laplanche reenvisions it in the context of the general theory of seduction, is aimed toward an object that is also the root of implanted sexuality (Laplanche also uses the term *aim-source-object*).[89] Following Laplanche, one is therefore led to envision not so much a loop but a spiral (if not an endless spiral) insofar as the object of the drive can never really be recaptured as such. The object must always be aimed for yet again, since the other in the

---

88 Quoted by Laplanche in *FBS*, p. 8.
89 *FBS*, p. 78.

primal situation is always characterized by his own source-objects, by his own unconscious. The question—already raised in *Life and Death*—of determining which is the true lost object, the object of need (milk) or the sexual object (breast), thus is at the same time both contained and surpassed in the framework of the translational model. As I have argued elsewhere, loss can be said to be inherent, from the outset, in the object itself[90]: it pertains to the fact that the object in question (which is the other) is affected by a hollow, the hollow of the other's own unconscious. The relation to this other can never permit a factual distinction between the object of need and the sexual object, insofar as one includes the other and ultimately they form a single object inevitably affected by the unconscious of the one who offers it to the child. The contrast with the theory of leaning-on is complete: for leaning-on, the lost object consists in the object of self-preservation, and the object of the sexual drive is derived from it by contiguity. Conversely, the general theory of seduction posits the object as compromised from the outset, as contaminated by unconscious sexual messages. The object is never in fact lost as an object of need (unless the very life of the infant is put in danger); but the object is *concurrently* an object that induces excitation and, as such, is always already lost.

At the beginning, then, we have a child with no unconscious who is confronted with adult messages compromised by the adult's unconscious sexuality; at the end we find a child endowed with a real unconscious, at once structural and dynamic, an unconscious that arises from primal repression conceived as a "failure of translation" in keeping with Freud's account in "Letter 52." In addition, this translational model revives, almost unchanged, the model of the *metabola* or *signifying substitution* advanced by Laplanche at the Bonneval Conference in 1960. Old Lacanian roots are thus discernible here, but they have been radically transformed, so that Laplanche's schema, derived

---

90 D. Scarfone, "'It Was *Not* My Mother': From Seduction to Negation." *New Formations* 48:69–76, 2002–2003.

from one of Lacan's, was "fiercely criticized, no doubt because it was at once too Lacanian and not Lacanian enough."[91] Here I cannot account for the model of metabola in detail and must settle for referring readers to Laplanche's original text.[92]

Let me stress that the translational model of repression is also related to a temporal dimension predicated on *après-coup*. The second stage of *après-coup* consists precisely in that moment of translation of a message that was registered but not translated in the first stage. In his letter to Fliess, Freud postulated several successive registrations, several transcriptions separated by translations, as well as by partial failures of translation. Laplanche returns to this model, pointing out that repression always comprises two dimensions: that of translation and that of repression, the latter representing the failure of the former. It would require much more space than I have here to explore the many theoretical and clinical implications of such a theorization of repression. However, lest the concept be reduced to a shallow factuality, let us be reminded by Laplanche that "the human being is, and will go on being, a self-translating and self-theorizing being. Primal repression is merely the first and founding moment in a life-long process."[93]

The Primal Situation and the Analytic Tub

Laplanche writes that between "infantile seduction (or 'early' seduction)" and "primal seduction" we are not moving "from the real to the 'mythical', for we have to reject this use of the term 'mythical' (or 'mythical time') by which some deliberately jettison the primal; the primal is a deepening of the notion of the real (human reality, naturally), revealing those ineluctable situations on which the real is

---

91 J. Laplanche, "A Short Treatise on the Unconscious," in *Essays on Otherness*, p. 93.
92 "The Unconscious: a Psychoanalytic Study" (1965 [1960]) in *The Unconscious and the Id*, Trans. Luke Thurston with Lindsay Watson, London: Rebus Press, 1999.
93 *NF*, p. 131.

founded: the primal is a category of effectivity, of *Wirklichkeit*."[94]

Among the situations able to establish and reestablish the primal, I will lay special emphasis on the "analytic situation" which was my starting point as I sought to find a path leading to foundations (see the section "Approaching the Primal" above). Equipped with the concept of the primal, I now return to the "analytic situation" and embark on a new cycle within a Laplanchian spiral. As it is itself a founding or refounding practice, within the analytic domain one necessarily finds, mutatis mutandi, all the constituents of the primal situation, and, in the foreground, the frame: rules that are not arbitrary but which from arise from "a set of inaugural gestures."[95] The treatment is a process of establishing, and of continual reestablishing. In *The Tub* (*Le baquet*),[96] Laplanche studies the delimitation of the analytic space at length: it is created by the suspension, the tangentialization of the realm of interests in order to set up *a purely drive-related or sexual sphere*. To the analysand, the analyst is the bearer of an enigma. Positioned as the one who is "supposed to know" (Lacan), the analyst not only must refuse to locate himself at the adaptational level, but he must also refuse and suspend knowledge. The analyst's *refusals* propel the analysis. But more fundamentally, as the bearer of the enigma in the analysand's view, the analyst sets up and reactivates, within the analysis, a primal seduction to which his *holding capacity* (*contenance*) further contributes.

If the analytic situation is a reopening, a revival, of the primal, it is because it includes an other. This inclusion will disrupt everything because it puts into play the enigma of the other—of the analyst. The relation to this enigma is what constitutes the transference. As a reinstatement of the primal, the situation as a whole is itself a process of transference—the transference of the primal—insofar as the analyst, through his offer of analysis, inevitably takes up the place of the

---

94 *NF*, p. 129 (translation modified).
95 *NF*, p. 160.
96 See "La situation analytique: Le psychanalyste et son baquet" ("The Analytic Situation: The Analyst and His Tub,"), in *P5*, pp. 7–134.

primal other whose enigmatic messages were directed at the child. Thus, as Laplanche puts it, the transference is provoked by the analyst.[97] Since it is itself a process of transference, how could the analytic situation claim to lead to a dissolution of the transference? Theorizing the end of analysis, Laplanche suggests a "transference of the transference." Such a transference of the transference may occur when, after completing a certain number of rotations (of translations)[98] around the axis of transference, the analysand arrives at a temporal window that permits his withdrawal from the orbit of the treatment, a window analogous to the one involved in the launching of spaceships. We see that Laplanche's set of metaphors, whether astronomical or astronautical, tends to spiral around a few permanent traits.

The transference of the analysand can be said to be "summoned" by the hollow of the analyst's enigma and his offer to analyze, a hollow maintained by the analyst's inner stance and refusals. The transference that occupies this hollow can itself either be hollowed-out (*en creux*) or filled-in (*en plein*). *Filled-in transference* consists in the most documented, traditional form of transference (the repetition of, say, what has already been translated and possibly repressed [secondary repression]). *Hollowed-out transference* occurs when, more fundamentally, the treatment becomes the site in which, pending a process of working through, the infantile situation is revived along with its enigmatic nature. Though Laplanche does not formulate it in these terms, I would say that the hollowed-out transference is what most specifically signals the reestablishment of the primal. In my view, this bears significant consequences for the possible revival of primal repression in severely traumatized patients.

It is in relation to this topic that Laplanche introduces a key distinction regarding the modalities of emergence of the adult sexual in the child: most fundamentally, primal seduction occasions an *implan-*

---

97 "Transference: Its Provocation by the Analyst," in *Essays on Otherness*, pp. 214–233.
98 Not to indulge in facile wordplay, it is pleasing to come across the word "translation" in this context.

tation of sexuality in the child, an implantation that the metaphor of a relation to the bodily surface best conveys. The translation-repression process occasioned by implantation of the enigmatic messages instigates a topographical differentiation: the subject creates a split between the unconscious and the preconscious-conscious in order to deal with the impossibility of fully translating the message of the other. Implantation would then involve the emergence of the sexual, a process that is undoubtedly traumatic, but traumatic in a way that leads to psychic structuring. Alongside implantation, or rather in contrast with that structuring form of emergence, Laplanche accounts for *intromission*, a violent variant of implantation that relates to the interior of the body. Intromission is an intrusion, the emergence of the sexual in a nonmetabolizable way that precludes the differentiation of psychic agencies. "While implantation allows the individual to take things up actively, at once translating and repressing, one must try to conceive of a process which blocks this, short-circuits the differentiation of the agencies in the process of their formation, and puts into the interior an element resistant to all metabolizing."[99]

Such a distinction seems to bring with it a basic heuristic value insofar as it permits thinking about what, within metapsychology itself, other authors (Winnicott, for example) might have explored in terms of *modifications*, not so much modifications of the treatment as modifications of a conceptualization that has often failed to be articulated in metapsychological terms. This applies, for instance, to borderline phenomena, "false-self organizations," "frozen affects," and "failures of mentalization," as well as to a number of psychotic states. Yet the distinction yields theoretical possibilities opening up a broad field of research for anyone willing to seize the opportunity. Viewing the treatment as a revival of the primal situation is more than a mere terminological reformulation. It has consequences for the conduct of the treatment, for the exploration of its potentialities and the institution of its ethics.

---

99 "Implantation, Intromission," in *Essays in Otherness*, p. 136 (translation modified).

But the distinction between implantation and intromission is not "strictly clinical" shorthand. As always, Laplanche weaves theory and clinical practice tightly in what he likes to call "the theoretic." Hence in the very step in which, with the notion of intromission, Laplanche seems to place the violent variant of implantation solely in the context of psychopathology, he at the same time opens up a research topic that applies to the entire theoretical field: "I have no doubt that a process related to intromission also has its role in the formation of the *superego,* a foreign body that cannot be metabolized."[100]

Radical Copernicanism

All in all, the development of Laplanche's thought has resolutely led him to a Copernican view of the human condition. The point is not to deny anyone the right to some Ptolemaic recentering, however. Just as, centuries after Copernicus, we carry on referring to sunset, each of us recenters around our ego, unaware of that "other thing" that continually subverts such narcissistic pride. But just as the beauty of the setting sun could never abolish the laws of astronomy, the ipsocentrism of human beings cannot eradicate the primacy of the other in everyone's psychic makeup. This other and this other's messages position the subject as a hermeneut, forcing him to interpret these messages, to fashion a version of them compatible with his ego, a version that accommodates his narcissism. This leads Laplanche to be critical of views that tend to situate psychoanalysis on the side of a hermeneutic model of interpretation. In short, Laplanche insists that the analyst *not* act as a hermeneut. The hermeneut epitomizes the human condition in general; the ego functions as a hermeneut when developing spontaneous theories, creating meaning, and organizing responses to anything coming from the other that causes

---

100 *Ibid.*

some reaction, even anxiety, and so prompts a process of translation. The attitude that flows from what is essential in the invention
of the analytic situation is constantly to swim against the current of
the spontaneous hermeneutics of humans, to carry out a process of
detranslation, of unbinding, bearing in mind that, as the translational
model reveals, every process of translation is the flip side of a process
of repression. Psychoanalysis is thus an antihermeneutic practice, not
only as a matter of principle or of method, but also in keeping with
the very idea of what makes up a human being at the outset: that
other that all forms of self-centered hermeneutics strive to obscure. In
Laplanche's view, modern hermeneuts, whether they are psychoanalysts or not, overlook the fact that hermeneutics originally consisted
in an effort to interpret the divine message: that is to say, once all con-
siderations of religious faith are set aside, to interpret words coming
from an other. If psychoanalysis has something new to offer on this
subject, it is its ability to reopen access to the primal other, accounting
for that other that dwells in direct opposition to the illusion of narcissistic autarky that stems from (among other things) the very capacity
to produce meaning.

Let us bear in mind that such narcissism is what Freud deemed
wounded by his discovery, as well as by that of Copernicus.[101] Yet,
the fact that individuals are constantly involved in a process of recentering around their narcissistic ego is replicated within the field of
psychoanalytic theory, as Freudian monadology itself entails the necessary subjective closure on oneself characteristic of all humans. It is
as if the same theory that wounded human narcissism had taken up
the task of repairing the damage. Does this imply that the attempt
to conceive of the other and his Copernican primacy as a center of
gravitation is inevitably doomed to fail? According to Laplanche, the

---

101 And by Darwin's discovery, though Laplanche points out that here the self-cen-
tering recentering is achieved much more easily: we might descend from apes, but
we can still see ourselves as the "pinnacle" of evolution. See "Ponctuation" in *RCI*,
pp. 32–33.

answer is "no," and the reason is that psychoanalysis is not only a theory tackling an object, it is also a method, indissolubly tied to the analytic situation. As I have noted, such a situation precisely revives the primal situation that characterizes all humans and thus reopens the ipsocentric narcissistic shell. As it turns out, the analytic situation is therefore both Ptolemaic and Copernican, involving an unending process of recentering and decentering in which, as opposed to Freud's famous motto that "there *ego* shall be," "where id was, the *other* will always and ever be."[102]

Laplanche's radical Copernicanism thus extends far beyond the field of psychoanalytic practice. In his view, the whole of Western philosophy has constantly reconstructed the human condition on an ego-centered basis; such a Ptolemaic closure needs to be countered at all times using concepts that are not ego-centered and through which the primal vector coming from the other is consistently underscored. This involves allo-centered concepts such as the concepts of revelation, persecution, and inspiration—this last leading Laplanche to put the theory of sublimation back to work.[103] In any case, as Freud stated with regard to neurotics, the point is to locate the ways in which the subject is somewhat right.[104] But once again, this applies far beyond the field of psychoanalytic clinical practice. One can never lay too much emphasis on this vector coming from the other, especially in this era when an exacerbated form of narcissism yields the gravest aberrations in the realms of both thought and act. One need only recall the implications, in recent history, of claims to ethnic purity, of the obtuse denial of the other, starting with the other within.

As it remains firmly aligned with a Copernican position,

---

102 *RCI*, p. 35.

103 In a personal exchange, Laplanche indicated his intention to revisit his reflection on sublimation from scratch, due to his dissatisfaction with the way he had tackled the subject in the third volume of the *Problématiques* series, which in his view was insufficiently Copernican.

104 "Seduction, Persecution, Revelation," in *Essays on Otherness*, pp. 166–196.

Laplanche's thought consequently carries an antimetaphysical position (the realism of the unconscious, the primacy of the other as the concrete, lower-case other), as well as an ethical stance regarding psychoanalysis (the analyst's refusals and respect for the enigma of his own unconscious), both of which lead to distinct generalizable philosophical stances. Laplanche first became involved with psychoanalysis as a philosopher in 1946–1947 because, in his view, psychoanalysis constituted the main path toward a renewal of the knowledge of mankind. In a relatively recent article in which he further explores the question of myth and shows how psychoanalysis, far from resorting to myth as a foundation, is in a position to account for the function of myth in what makes up a human being, he makes a bold plea for a broadening of metapsychology, toward the advent of an "indispensable meta-anthropology."[105]

The time has now come to reach a conclusion. I have provided an overview of Laplanche's thought in which, because a full account of it cannot possibly be given in this short work, one axis has been privileged. Suited to the purpose of expounding key aspects of Laplanche's thought, this axis captures the *movement* that drives his thought. This movement has the form of a spiral or helix, consisting in an orbital motion around a decentered center. Yet let us not be overly reassured by this analogy with Copernican heliocentrism. Indeed, the kind of decentering Laplanche insists on does not allow us to think, as Copernicus did regarding the sun, that the core of the problem has simply been shifted from *self* (*ipse*) to an *other* posited as a "clear center." The kind of enigma evoked by Laplanche might well arise from the other, but it is enigmatic for this other as well. If I may indulge in one last reference to astronomy, I will finally mention Kepler, who described elliptical orbits featuring two centers, not one: the sun and a second center that remains forever obscure.

---

105 "La psychanalyse, entre mythe et théorie," in *Revue philosophique*, no. 2, 1997; rep. *Revue française de psychanalyse* LXII, 1998, no. 3, pp. 871–388.

Postscript

For a while, I thought that this final image of an obscure center was a personal contribution, an addition to Laplanche's astronomical metaphors. But as he reminds us with Hölderlin, a river always flows in the direction of its source. Hölderlin is the poet about whom Laplanche wrote his dissertation[106] when he was a medical student, a dissertation celebrated by Foucault at the time it was published. I have not said much about this first book by Laplanche and would be sorry not to devote at least a few lines to it, especially in light of the fact that, as I was looking through it—precisely out of regret for having omitted it—I discovered that my work too was flowing, unbeknownst to me, in the direction of a source. Indeed, I was just concluding with the sun and an obscure center, and here is what Laplanche writes in the very last lines of *Hölderlin:*

> The image of nightfall, of the *Umnachtung,* frequently comes to the mind of those who approach the poetic life of Hölderlin in the years 1800–1806. Certain critics see him trying to take advantage of the final glimmer of daylight; others think that he is describing this twilight, or that his poetic abilities are increased tenfold by the emotion that accompanies this tragic hour. I would see him rather, at the moment when he is reached by the cone of shadow projected by the earth, as racing against it—not by running away from the shadow but by heading straight for the sun. But we would have to reverse everything in this image, as in a photographic negative in which the sun is black.[107]

The reader was forewarned: Jean Laplanche is an interstellar traveler in the universe of the soul. Will his spaceship sail out of the solar system?

---

106 *Hölderlin and the Question of the Father,* Victoria, Canada, ELS Editions, 2007.
107 *Op. cit.,* p. 118 (translation modified).

PRIMAL FANTASY, FANTASIES OF ORIGINS, ORIGINS OF FANTASY

(1964)

PRIMAL FANTASY,
FANTASIES OF ORIGINS,
ORIGINS OF FANTASY[1]
(1964)

Postscript (1985)

This text, like all psychoanalytic texts but perhaps more than others, is dated. By "dated" we do not mean that twenty years after its first publication in *Les Temps Modernes* it has become obsolete. At least we hope not, as much for today's reader as for ourselves. But, incontestably, it is time-stamped both by the circumstances of its publication and by its rhythm.

---

1 Translator's note: In the first English translation the title *"Fantasme Originaire, Fantasmes des Origines, Origines du Fantasme"* was rendered "Fantasy and Origins of Sexuality" (*International Journal of Psychoanalysis* 49:1-18, 1968), a choice that underlines what may be the essay's most important contribution but that sacrifices the playfulness of the original. This is a consistent choice of that earlier translation and, in my view, more is lost than wordplay. Although a discussion of its significance is beyond the scope of a footnote, the fact that this essay was first published not in a psychoanalytic journal but in *Les Temps Modernes* gives the context for the text's style, which is both conversational and learned, forthright and nuanced, playful and precise. When I have seen a choice between possibly confusing richness and possibly misleading clarity, I opted for the former. (See, for example, footnote 5.) In general I have tried to retain the authors' provocations and playfulness. This is not simply a matter of style nor a question of accessibility. Rather I have tried to respect the authors' principled refusal, following the example of Freud, to force their thinking onto the procrustean bed of academic/scientific style.

We wrote it with a sense of urgency, an urgency attributable first of all to an act of rupture. In 1964 we had just announced our refusal to follow Lacan into what was called "l'École" and would become *his* école, but we could not allow ourselves to fully recognize that we had already distanced ourselves from his thought. As a result, there is in this short essay an oscillation between audacity and prudence, an oscillation also felt in the rhythm of the writing: sometimes proceeding slowly, step by step, but often condensing excessively. In creating a "return to Freud" entirely in our own way, we demonstrated our refusal to buy a one-way ticket to Lacan. Yet at the same time we remained quite concerned to establish a continuity between Freud and Lacan.

Our study is time-stamped also in that it was written on the heels of *The Language of Psycho-analysis,* which at the time was almost finished. No doubt it could be said that, like that work, this essay is a kind of exegesis, but only if exegesis is understood as letting one's own thinking be enriched by a thought as sovereign as it is enigmatic, and not the exploitation of a heritage rehashed all too often.

Discovery of a treasure includes a time of astonishment before a time of inventory—then the necessary squandering. Let us remember: the richness of the Freudian lexicon was barely suspected by those who, at the time, contented themselves with living on its income; that is, when they didn't give a single Other the task of proclaiming its Truth.

First we had to bring back to light some completely forgotten concepts (forgotten from the beginning by the Freudians, even by Freud himself). Concepts such as "leaning-on" ["anaclisis"[2]] and "primal fantasy." We had to restore full and foundational—if not transcenden-

---

2 Translator's note: In the *Standard Edition* "anaclisis" was used to translate the ordinary German word *anlehnung* (translated as *étayage* in French). In more recent translations "propped upon," "leaning," and "leaning-on" have been used. In UIT's collection of translations of works by and about Laplanche "s'étayage" is translated by "leaning-on" or "leaning," emphasizing the drive's activity, its agency.

tal—value to notions reduced to banalities, such as "autoerotism," and to those discredited and misunderstood like "seduction."

Soon the task became more difficult, as we were torn between two imperatives: neither to falsify nor schematize Freud's thought, but to attempt to restore its demands, its repressions and returns, its ambiguities, perhaps its "naivetés" (e.g., the phylogenetic hypothesis); and, on the other hand, to advance our own project of laying out a more explicit, coherent, and stimulating configuration.

Which is to say that the reader—and we ourselves, in rereading our work—will detect many levels in this text:

- a necessary and healthy archaeology of concepts that strives to be both faithful and critical;

- an attempt at interpretation of the problematic of origins, in which a structuralist inspiration remains perceptible despite our denials;

- and, finally, the germs of new developments that each of us would later pursue more freely, each affirming his choice within the psychoanalytic experience whose fields Freud had marked out and plowed.

At least we have taken the risk of reopening and unfolding within the field of the "sexual" in psychoanalysis the question of "infantile" origins, a question which, if it has no citizenship in positivist knowledge, must haunt our thought: that of the psychoanalyst and that of the philosopher, who here try to walk in step.

Reread today, republished without modification—except that chapter titles have been added, some notes integrated into the body of the text, and references made precise—for us, this essay retains the value of an index: the finger that points to a thing, the gesture that extends itself in a path requiring detours, the sign of a riddle and not its solution.

"I used to visit her in the evening"

From its origins, psychoanalysis has brewed the material of fantasies. In the inaugural case of Anna O., Breuer seems to do nothing but intrude into the world of the patient's imaginary productions, in her "private theater," in order to allow a catharsis by way of verbalization and expression of emotion. "I used to visit her in the evening," he tells us, "when I knew I should find her in her hypnosis, and then I relieved her of the whole stock of imaginative products which she had accumulated since my last visit."[3] Reading this case, one is struck by how, in contrast to Freud, Breuer has little interest in retrieving actual lived experiences that might be at the root of the daydreams. In the events that are understood as initiators of neurosis, there is already an element of the imaginary, a hallucination, which causes the trauma. There is a circular relationship between the fantasy and the dissociation of consciousness that results in the formation of a unconscious kernel: the fantasy becomes traumatic when it occurs on the basis of a special state, described as "hypnoid," but inversely the fantasy, by the fright and stupefaction it provokes, contributes to the creation of this fundamental state; there is "autohypnosis."

If Breuer puts himself in an imaginary world and tries to reduce its pathogenic power without referring to anything extrinsic, is that any different from the practice of certain contemporary analysts, particularly the followers of Melanie Klein? From the start, the imaginary dramas that underlie the verbal or behavioral material brought into the session by the patient are made explicit and verbalized (here probably by the analyst): introjection and projection of fantasized breast or penis, intrusions, struggles or compromises of good and bad objects, etc.[4] The progress of the treatment, if it ends in a better

---

3 J. Breuer and S. Freud (1895), *Studies on Hysteria, Standard Edition* II, p. 30.
4 M. Klein (1960), *Narrative of a Child Psycho-Analysis.*

adaptation to reality, is not expected to arise from any corrective method but from a dialectic in which fantasies are integrated to the extent that they are revealed; in the final analysis, the stable introjection of the good object (no less imaginary than the bad object) allows a fusion of the instincts in an equilibrium based on dominance of the libido over the death instinct.

In German the word *Phantasie* is the term used to designate the imagination, not so much the faculty of imagining (the philosophers' *Einbildungskraft*) as the imaginary world and its contents: the imaginings or fantasies into which the neurotic and the poet gladly retreat. In these scenes that the subject recounts, or that the analyst tells him, the hint of a séance is impossible to ignore. How then can one resist the temptation to define this imaginary world of fantasy in opposition to what it separates itself from: the world of reality? This opposition long preceded psychoanalysis, but from the start there is the risk that the theory and practice of psychoanalysis will be shut up within these terms.

In theoretical work, how have psychoanalysts handled this? Quite badly, and most often by relying on the crudest theories of knowledge.

Melanie Klein—whose technique is free of all orthopedic[5] aims and who, more than any other, has sought to distinguish the contingent imagery of daydreams from the structural function and permanence of what she calls "unconscious phantasies"[6]—in the end has to maintain that those "unconscious phantasies" are "false perceptions." For us, the "good object" and the "bad object" must rig-

---

5 Translator's note: Here the French text has *orthopédique* which is as provocative in French as it is in English. The *Oxford English Dictionary* defines "orthopedic" as "relating to or concerned with the cure of deformities in children or of bodily deformities in general."
6 Further on we will discuss this distinction.

orously be placed in quotation marks,[7] even if the entire development of the subject takes place within them.

And Freud? In the course of this study we will see all the ambiguity of his theorizing, and how at each bend of his thinking he finds another open path. However, if we first take up his doctrine in its most official version, the world of fantasies seems to lie completely within the frame of the opposition between subjective and objective, between an interior world that tends to find satisfaction in illusion and an exterior world, mediated by the perceptual system, that progressively imposes the reality principle on the subject. The unconscious, then, appears as the inheritor of what initially was the subject's only world, a world governed by the pleasure principle alone. The world of fantasies is akin to the "nature reserves" that civilized nations create to perpetuate the state of nature. "With the introduction of the reality principle one species of thought-activity was split off; it was kept free from reality testing and remained subordinated to the pleasure principle alone. This activity is fantasying. . . ." [8] Unconscious processes "entirely disregard reality testing; they equate reality of thought with external reality, and wishes with their fulfillment—with the event."[9] This absence of "standards of reality" in the unconscious threatens to mark it as a lesser entity, a less differentiated state.

---

7 "Good" and "bad" objects are "imagos which are a phantastically distorted picture of the real objects upon which they are based" (Melanie Klein). [Translator's note: The source of this quotation is uncertain but approximately the same notion can be found in Klein's *On Criminality* (1934), in which she says, "The small child first harbors against its parents aggressive impulses and phantasies, it then projects these on to them, and thus it comes about that it develops a phantastic and distorted picture of the people around it. But the mechanism of introjection operates at the same time, so that these unreal imagos become internalized, with the result that the child feels itself to be ruled by phantastically dangerous and cruel parents—the super-ego within itself" (*Love, Guilt and Reparation & Other Works 1921–1945*, pp. 258–259.]

8 S. Freud (1911), *Two Principles of Mental Functioning, Standard Edition* XII, p. 222. [Translator's note: The sentence quoted continues, "which begins already in children's play, and later, continued as *day-dreaming*, abandons dependence on real objects."]

9 *Ibid.*, p. 225.

In psychoanalytic practice any conceptual weakness will produce an effect. If only for the record we should mention all techniques which, relying on the opposition between the imaginary and the real, in the end propose to perfect the integration of the pleasure principle with the reality principle, a path on which the neurotic has gone only half way? Of course, it is a bit unusual to call on "realities" outside the analysis; the material must be analyzed within the patient's relation to the analyst, "in the transference." But, if we don't watch out, any transference interpretation—"You are acting with me as if . . ."—will insinuate: "And you know very well that, in reality, I am not who you think I am"?

Fortunately, technique saves us: we don't articulate that unhappy implication.[10] More radically, the analytic rule should be understood as epoché,[11] absolute suspension of all judgments of reality. Isn't that how we put ourselves on the same level as the unconscious, which makes no such judgments? A patient tells us he is an adopted child. He recounts fantasies in which, searching for his real mother, he realizes that she is a society woman turned prostitute. Don't we recognize the banal theme of the "family romance" that a child who has *not* been adopted might forge? Within this phenomenological reduction, there is no need to distinguish the two cases, except to denounce as *defense by reality* the support the patient found in his adoption documents. The suspension of reference to reality becomes a "That's what *you* say," which pushed to a derogatory limit becomes "That is all subjective."

And yet in the case of the real adoption to which we allude, the difference emerges on the clinical level: enactment, rapidly blunted, of fantasies of reunion with the mother, episodes where the attempt

---

10 It is admirable to see how Melanie Klein, who interprets the transference in a continuous flow, succeeds in never raising the "in reality" or even the "as if."

11 Translator's note: The Greek word—εποχή—is defined as a *check* or *cessation*; for example, the *epoch* of a star is the point at which it seems to halt after reaching the zenith (Plutarch).

to rejoin the *true* mother is symbolically enacted in a sort of a daze, etc. From the beginning of the treatment, numerous elements showed the disjunction between the raw reality and speech—dream contents, repeated occurrences of sleeping in session—manifested a regressive tendency toward the origins

Haunted—and who can blame him?—by the need to know what region of being he is wandering in, Freud does not offer a convincing justification for the suspension of reference to reality during treatment. At first he feels almost a duty to show the patient all his cards. But captured, like the patient himself, within the "real or imaginary" alternative, how could he evade the double risk either of losing the analysand's interest at the beginning should he learn that all his productions are only imaginings (*Einbildungen*), or of being reproached later on for having encouraged the patient to take fantasies for realities?[12] At this point, the solution Freud invokes is "psychic reality"—a new dimension at first not accessible to the analysand. But what is this idea? What does Freud mean by "psychic reality"?

Often nothing more than the reality of our thoughts, of our inner world, a reality that is at least as important as that of the material world, and whose effects are decisive for neurotic phenomena.[13] If by this we are contrasting the reality of psychological phenomena with "material reality," the "reality of thought" with "external actuality,"[14] then it comes down to saying that we are working within

---

12 S. Freud (1917), *Introductory Lectures on Psycho-Analysis, Standard Edition* XVI: "[The patient] too wants to experience realities and despises everything that is merely 'imaginary'. If, however, we leave him, till this piece of work is finished, in the belief that we are occupied in investigating real events of his childhood, we run the risk of his later on accusing us of being mistaken and laughing at us for our apparent credulity. It will be a long time before he can take in our proposal that we should equate phantasy and reality and not bother to begin with whether the childhood experiences under examination are the one or the other" (p. 368).

13 *Ibid*. "The phantasies possess *psychical* reality as contrasted with *material* reality, and we gradually learn to understand that *in the world of the neuroses it is psychical reality which is the decisive kind*" (p. 368).

14 S. Freud (1911), *Two principles... Standard Edition* XII, p. 225.

the imaginary, within the subjective; the subjective is our object. It is the object of psychology and is as worthy as the objects of the natural sciences. Doesn't the very term psychic *reality* show that Freud could only confer the dignity of being an object on psychological phenomena by reference to material reality, by affirming that "they too possess a reality of a sort"?[15] The suspension of the standards of reality, in the absence of a new category, pushes us back to the "reality" of the purely subjective.

And yet... When he introduces this notion of psychic reality, in the last lines of *The Interpretation of Dreams*, where he summarizes the whole thesis (a dream is not a phantasmagoria but a text to be deciphered), Freud does not define it as *all* of the subjective, like the domain of psychology, but as a heterogeneous core in this domain, resistant and, alone among psychological phenomena, truly "real." "Whether we are to attribute *reality* to unconscious wishes, I cannot say. It must be denied, of course, to any transitional or intermediate thoughts. If we look at unconscious wishes reduced to their most fundamental and truest shape, we shall have to conclude, no doubt, that *psychical* reality is a particular form of existence not to be confused with *material* reality."[16]

So, we are given three kinds of phenomena (of reality in the larger sense): material reality, the reality of "transitional or intermediate thoughts"[17] (psychological thoughts), and the reality of unconscious desire and its "truest expression" (fantasy).

As for "psychic reality," a new category constantly obscured in Freud's writing, it won't do to begin by designating it as "the symbolic" or "the structural." If Freud keeps finding and losing this

---

15 S. Freud (1917), *Introductory lectures... Standard Edition* XVI, p. 368.
16 *Standard Edition* V, p. 620. Freud's rewriting of this passage in the course of successive editions of the dream book (reviewed in the note on p. 620) shows both Freud's worry about defining psychic reality and the difficulty he had doing it.
17 *Standard Edition* V, p. 620.

"psychic reality," it is not merely the consequence of a deficiency in his conceptual tools; rather, the relation of "psychic reality" to the real and to the imaginary, a relation that itself is structural, creates the ambiguity and difficulty that arise in the central domain of fantasy.

One more word about the epoché, the suspension of the judgment of reality, expressed in the analytic rule: "Speak everything, but do no more than speak." The rule is not suspension of the reality of external events *for the sake of* subjective reality. Rather, the rule creates a new domain, that of speaking, in which the difference between the real and the imaginary can remain important (see the case of the adopted patient). The homology between the analytic domain and the domain of the unconscious is based not on their common "subjectivity" but in the profound kinship of the unconscious with the domain of speech. It's not "So *you* say" but "So you *say*."

"I no longer believe in my neurotica"

The years of psychoanalytic discovery, 1895–1899, are important as much for the questionable character of the struggle that led to the discoveries as for the oversimplified way the history is typically written.

For example, if one reads Ernst Kris's introduction to the *Origins of Psychoanalysis*,[18] the evolution of Freud's views seems perfectly clear: the facts—most notably his self-analysis—forced him to abandon his initial ideas; the *scene of seduction* by the adult, which until then was his prototype for psychic trauma, is not a real event but a fantasy that is itself only the product and the disguise of spontaneous expressions of infantile sexuality. When writing about his own history, doesn't Freud confirm this version?

---

18 Especially Chapter III, "Infantile Sexuality and Self-Analysis," pp. 27–34 in *The Origins of Psychoanalysis; Sigmund Freud's letters to Wilhelm Fliess*, ed. Marie Bonaparte, Anna Freud, and Ernst Kris. New York: Basic Books, 1954.

If hysterical subjects trace back their symptoms to traumas that are fictitious, then the new fact which emerges
is precisely that they create such scenes in *phantasy,* and
this psychical reality requires to be taken into account
alongside practical reality. This reflection was soon followed by the discovery that these phantasies were
intended to cover up the auto-erotic activity of the first
years of childhood, to embellish it and raise it to a higher
plane. And now, from behind the phantasies, the whole
range of a child's sexual life came to light.[19]

Freud admits his "error": he had at first imputed to the "outside" what has to do with the "inside."

Seduction *theory*—the word alone should give us pause: it
is the elaboration of an explanatory model for the etiology of certain neuroses and not purely clinical observation of the frequency
of seduction of children by adults, or even the simple *hypothesis* that
such seductions play a dominant role in the series of traumatic events.
Freud's concern is to establish as a rule the connection he discovered
between sexuality, trauma, and defense: to show that it is in the very
nature of sexuality to have a traumatic effect and, inversely, that ultimately one can speak of trauma as the origin of neurosis only insofar
as there has been sexual seduction. When Freud maintained this thesis
(in the years 1895–1897), the role of defensive conflict in the genesis of
hysteria, and of the "neuropsychoses of defense" in general, was fully
recognized without minimizing the etiological function of trauma.
Notions of defense and trauma are tightly connected to one another.
The seduction theory, in showing how only sexual trauma has the
power to launch a "pathologic defense" (repression), is an attempt to
account for the fact, discovered in clinical work (*Studies on Hysteria*),
that repression acts selectively on sexuality.

---

19 S. Freud (1914), "On the History of the Psychoanalytic Movement," *Standard Edition* XIV, pp. 17–18.

Let's stop for a moment to examine the schema proposed by Freud. The process of psychic trauma is broken up into several moments and always requires *at least two events*. In the first, "the scene of seduction," the child is subjected to a sexual approach by an adult (an attack or advance), which does not arouse any sexual excitement in the child. To consider such a scene traumatic would require abandoning the somatic model of trauma: there is no flood of external excitation nor are the child's "defenses" overwhelmed. It can be considered sexual only insofar as it is seen from the outside by the adult. In contrast, the child has neither the bodily potential for sexual excitement nor the mental representations needed to integrate the event. Sexual in itself, the event cannot have a sexual meaning for the child: it is "pre-sexual sexual."[20] As for the second event, which occurs after puberty, one could say it is even more nontraumatic than the first. It is nonviolent and seemingly harmless; its only power lies in retroactively evoking the first event due to some associated features.

Thus, it is the memory of the first scene that triggers sexual excitation, catching the "ego" from behind and leaving it powerless, in no condition to use defenses normally directed toward the outer world, and therefore giving rise to a "pathological defense," a "posthumous primary process": the memory is repressed.

If we return to conceptions that may at first appear to have only historical interest because they seem to presuppose an innocent child, without sexuality, and thus to contradict undeniable later findings, it is not simply to trace the stages of a discovery.

In our eyes, this explanatory schema, which Freud called a *proton pseudos*,[21] retains value as a model for understanding human

---

20 Freud to Fliess, October 15, 1895: "Have I revealed the great clinical secret to you, either orally or in writing? Hysteria is the consequence of a pre-sexual *sexual shock*. Obsessional neurosis is the consequence of a pre-sexual *sexual pleasure* which is later transformed into [self-] reproach" *(The Complete Letters of Sigmund Freud to Wilhelm Fliess*, ed. J.M. Masson, Cambridge: Harvard University Press, 1985).

21 Proton pseudos – πρῶτον ψεῦδος - literally 'first lie' a concept of Aristotelian logic referring to the first false premise in a deduction.

sexuality—valuable for the difficulty that thinking about the schema entails. It puts in play two major formulations. On one hand—in a first phase—sexuality literally bursts in from outside, breaking into and entering a "childhood world" presumed to be innocent, in which sexuality becomes encysted as a raw event without provoking a defensive reaction: by itself, this event is not pathogenic. On the other hand—in a second phase—after the physiological sexual awakening of puberty, displeasure is produced and the origin of this displeasure is sought in the memory of the first event, an external event transformed into an inside event, an internal " foreign body" that now erupts within the subject.

Already in *Studies on Hysteria,* one finds the idea that psychic trauma is not reducible to the impressions made, once and for all, by an external event. "The causal relation between the determining psychical trauma and the hysterical phenomenon is not of a kind implying that the trauma merely acts like an *agent provocateur* in releasing the symptom, which thereafter leads an independent existence. We must presume rather that the psychical trauma—or more precisely the memory of the trauma—acts like a foreign body which long after its entry must be regarded as an agent that is still at work. . . ."[22]

A surprising answer to the question posed by psychic trauma: is it, on the model of a penetrating wound, an influx of external excitation that traumatizes the subject or, on the contrary, is it internal excitation, a drive which, lacking an outlet, puts the subject into a "state of helplessness"?[23] With the seduction theory, one can say that *as a whole* psychic trauma comes from both outside and inside. From outside because sexuality arrives in the subject[24] from *the other;* from

---

22 *Standard Edition* II, p. 6.

23 This problematic is present throughout such works as *Beyond the Pleasure Principle* and "Inhibitions, Symptoms and Anxieties," as well as Rank's *The Trauma of Birth.*

24 "It seems to me more and more that the essential point of hysteria is that it results from *perversion* on the part of the seducer, and *more and more* that heredity is seduction by the father." Freud, letter of December 6, 1896, in *The Complete Letters of Sigmund Freud to Wilhelm Fliess,* op. cit., p. 212; and letter #52 in *Standard Edition* I, pp. 238–239.

inside because it pours forth from this internalized externality, this "reminiscence" from which, according to the lovely formula, hysterics suffer, and in which we can already recognize fantasy.

This model of psychic trauma coming from both outside and inside is a seductive solution, but it risks collapsing as soon as one permits the meaning of each term slip: the "outside" toward the event, the "inside" toward the endogenous and the biological.

From the other direction, let's try to look for what's best in the seduction theory, to save what it offers at its deepest level. This is Freud's first and only attempt to establish an intrinsic relation between repression and sexuality.[25] He finds the dynamism of this relation not in any "content" but in the temporal characteristics of human sexuality, which make it the privileged domain of a dialectic between too much and too little excitation, and between the too soon and too late of the event: "Here, indeed, the one possibility is realized of a memory having greater releasing power subsequently than had been produced by the experience corresponding to it."[26] Hence the splitting of psychic trauma into two moments; psychic trauma can only be conceived as coming from something already there: the reminiscence of the first scene.

How then can we conceive of the formation of that "already there"? How did the first "pre-sexual sexual" scene acquire meaning for the subject? In a perspective that reduces the temporal dimension to chronology, one either falls into an infinite regress— every scene becoming sexual only by evoking an earlier scene without which it would have been *nothing* for the subject—or one stops arbitrarily at a "first" scene in spite of what then becomes inexplicable about it.

---

25 See "An Outline of Psychoanalysis" (1938), *Standard Edition* XXIII, pp. 185–186. Freud never stopped asserting this relation.

26 Draft K, *Standard Edition* I, p. 221. [Translator's note: The passage continues, "Only one thing is necessary for this: that puberty should be interpolated between the experience and its repetition in memory . . . ."]

An illusion: the doctrine of an innocent childhood world into which sexuality is introduced from outside by a perverse adult! An illusion, or rather a myth whose very contradictions attest its nature. We must conceive of a child who is "before" sexuality, a *bon sauvage*, and, at the same time, within the child, a sexuality "already there"— at least sexual in itself —so that it can be awakened; and we must reconcile an intrusion from the outside into an inside with the idea that perhaps, before this intrusion, there was no "inside," reconcile the passivity of simply submitting to a meaning imposed from the outside, with the minimum activity necessary for an experience to be received, and reconcile the indifference of innocence with the disgust that seduction is supposed to provoke. In a phrase, a subject before subjectivity receiving its being, its sexual being, from an outside before the distinction between inside and outside.

Forty years later Ferenczi took up the seduction theory and gave it an analogous importance.[27] His formulations may be less rigorous than Freud's but they have the virtue of perfecting the myth with two essential elements: beyond the events but through their mediation a new "language," the language of "passion," is introduced by the adult into the infantile "language" of "tenderness." This language of passion is the language of desire, necessarily marked by the forbidden, by guilt, and by hatred: a language in which the feeling of annihilation is linked to the pleasure of orgasm. The child's fantasy of the primal scene with its characteristic violence is evidence of the introjection of adult erotism.

From the start Freud rejected the banal thesis which attributes the displeasure provoked by sexuality to an external prohibition. Whether of "internal" or "external" origin, desire and the forbidden march in step: "We shall be plunged deep into psychological riddles if we enquire into the origin of the unpleasure which seems to be released

---

27 S. Ferenczi (1933), "Confusion of Tongues between Adults and the Child," in *Final Contributions to the Problems and Methods of Psycho-Analysis*, pp. 156–167. London: Karnac Books, 1994.

by premature sexual stimulation and without which, after all, a repression cannot be explained. The most plausible answer will appeal to the fact that shame and morality are the repressing forces and that the neighbourhood in which the sexual organs are naturally placed must inevitably arouse disgust along with sexual experiences. . . . I do not think that the release of unpleasure during sexual experiences is the consequence of the chance admixture of certain unpleasurable factors. . . . In my opinion there must be an independent source for the release of unpleasure in sexual life: once that source is present, it can activate sensations of disgust, lend force to morality, and so on."[28]

Just like Freud in 1895, Ferenczi is forced to situate this intrusion chronologically and to hypostasize a child before seduction. Inversely, one may be tempted to decide the question once and for all by invoking the domain of myth: seduction would be a myth, a myth in which the origin of sexuality is the introjection of the desire, the fantasies, and the "language" of adults. The relation of myth to time (to the event), mentioned in the myth itself, seems to be surrounded by the myth. But how can we stop there? The myth (or the fantasy) of the intrusion of the fantasy (or myth) into the subject must itself occur at some point in the life of the little human, a point at which, as a function of his biological development, we can already read the too much and the too little, the too soon (birth) and the too late (puberty).

During 1897, Freud renounced his seduction theory. On September 21 he wrote to Fliess: "And now I want to confide in you immediately the great secret that has been slowly dawning on me in the last few months. I no longer believe in my *neurotica*." He makes a number of arguments. Arguments of fact: the impossibility of bringing analyses to a conclusion, that is, all the way to the first pathogenic event; even in the most severe psychoses—which is to say states in which the unconscious seems most accessible—the answer to the riddle does not appear. Arguments of logic: the incidence of perver-

---

28 Draft K, *Standard Edition* I, pp. 221–222.

sion among fathers would have to be far greater than the incidence of hysteria, because the creation of hysteria requires additional factors. Besides, and this above all is what interests us, "there are no indications of reality in the unconscious, so that one cannot distinguish one from the other; between truth and fiction invested with affect." Two paths toward a solution are open: to see in the infantile fantasies only the retroactive projection of a reconstruction created by the adult (this will become the Jungian concept of *Zurückphantasieren,* which Freud rejected immediately); or to go back to the idea of an hereditary predisposition. If this second possibility—which Freud admitted he had always "repressed"—gains ground, it is certainly because searching for a first event has led to a dead end; but it is also because Freud, in this time of confusion, could not disentangle what was positive in the seduction theory apart from the realism of a datable event. If the event slips away, the other alternative—constitution—is rehabilitated. Since the real, in one of its respects, crumbles and reveals itself as merely "fiction," we need to look elsewhere for a real that creates this fiction.

When the historians of psychoanalysis, repeating the official line of Freud himself, tell us that Freud, by facing facts and abandoning the seduction theory, cleared the ground for the discovery of infantile sexuality, they simplify a much more ambiguous evolution. For contemporary psychoanalysts, for Ernst Kris as for us, infantile sexuality is inseparable from the Oedipus complex. And it is clear that, simultaneously with abandonment of the seduction theory, three themes become prominent in the correspondence with Fliess: infantile sexuality, fantasy, Oedipus. But the key problem is how they are articulated. So what do we see? If the reality of trauma and the scene of seduction have been cleared away,[29] to the extent that they were causal they are replaced not by Oedipus but by a spontaneous infantile sexuality whose development is essentially endogenous. Stages of evolution,

---

29 It would be easy to demonstrate that throughout his life Freud continued to emphasize the reality of real episodes of seduction.

fixation conceived as inhibition of development, and genetic regression—that is at least one of the perspectives offered in *Three Essays on Sexuality*, a work whose second chapter, "Infantile Sexuality," mentions neither Oedipus nor fantasy. An article contemporaneous with the first edition of *Three Essays* is important in this respect: Freud can speak of his "views on the part played by sexuality in the aetiology of the neuroses" *without saying a single word* about the Oedipus complex. The child's sexual development is defined as endogenous, as determined by the "sexual constitution": "Accidental influences derived from experience having thus receded into the background, the factors of constitution and heredity necessarily gained the upper hand once more; but there was this difference between my views and those prevailing in other quarters, that on my theory the 'sexual constitution' took the place of a 'general neuropathic disposition.'"[30]

Yet, one could object, it was also in 1897, precisely when he abandoned the seduction theory, that Freud, in his self-analysis, discovered the Oedipus complex. Nevertheless, consider this: in Freud's writings, over a twenty-year period, despite an importance recognized from the start, the Oedipus complex had only a marginal existence in Freud's theoretical syntheses; for example, it is deliberately isolated in the section on the choice of objects at puberty (*Three Essays*) and in a section on "typical dreams" in *Interpretation of Dreams*. As we see it, the discovery of the Oedipus conflict in 1897 was neither the cause of the abandonment of the seduction theory nor what took its place. It is much better understood as something that, having already been reached in "primitive" form in the seduction theory, nearly disappeared along with it and was replaced by biological realism.

Moreover, Freud himself recognized—but only much later— what was positive and precocious, in the seduction theory: in 1925 "I had stumbled for the first time upon the Oedipus complex";[31] in 1938

---

30 *Standard Edition* VII, pp. 275–276.
31 *An Autobiographical Study*, Standard Edition XX, p. 34.

"I came to understand that hysterical symptoms are derived from phantasies and not from real occurrences. It was only later that I was able to recognize in this phantasy of being seduced by the father the expression in a woman of the typical Oedipus complex."[32]

During an extended period, losing the notion, present in the seduction theory, of a "foreign body" that introduces the mark of human sexuality into the subject, and also discovering that the sexual drive does not wait for puberty to become active, Freud could not connect one with the other, Oedipus with infantile sexuality. From that moment on, if infantile sexuality exists—as observation and clinical work undeniably demonstrate—it can be conceptualized only as a biological reality, and fantasy nothing more than the secondary expression of that reality. The scene in which the subject describes himself as seduced by an older child is in fact doubly disguised: a pure fantasy is converted into a real memory, and spontaneous sexual activity is transformed into a scene of passivity.[33] At this point there is scarcely any basis to see fantasy as psychic reality—in the rigorous sense Freud sometimes assigns the term—since reality is entirely *given back* to endogenous sexuality, of which the fantasies are only a purely imaginary efflorescence.

With the abandonment of the seduction theory, something is lost: in the conjunction of and the temporal play between two "scenes" a presubjective structure asserts itself, a structure beyond both the specific event and the internal imagery. Prisoner of a series of conceptual alternatives—subject/object, constitution/event, internal/external, imaginary/real—for a while Freud was led to give weight to the first term in each of these "pairs of opposites."

So we have arrived at the following paradox: at the very

---

32 *New Introductory Lectures, Standard Edition* XXII, p. 120.

33 "I have learned to explain a number of phantasies of seduction as attempts at fending off memories of the subject's own sexual activity (infantile masturbation)." In "My Views on the Part Played by Sexuality in the Aetiology of the Neuroses," *Standard Edition* VII, p. 274.

moment that fantasy, the quintessential object of psychoanalysis, is discovered, it is at risk of seeing its fundamental substance replaced by an endogenous reality, a sexuality that is itself wrestling with external reality—a prohibitory and normative external reality that imposes disguises. Of course, we still have fantasy in the sense of imaginary production, but we lose the structure. Inversely, with the seduction theory we had, if not the hypothesis of the structure, at least the *intuition* of it (seduction appearing as a quasi-universal fact, in any case transcending the event and, so to speak, the actors), but fantasy's productive powers were unknown, or at least underestimated.

"I read prehistory"

It would be a blinkered account to limit the evolution of Freud's thinking around 1897 to this: going from an historical foundation for symptoms to a theory that ultimately is biological and can be summarized as a causal sequence:

sexual constitution → fantasy → symptom

Freud never fully adopts this theory except when forced to present his etiological "views" systematically. If one were to follow the history of Freud's thinking step by step, which is not our purpose here, we would have to point out at least two additional currents in this pivotal period.

One current at work from 1896 flows from the new discoveries about fantasy: fantasies are not only material to analyze—whether those immediately understood as fiction (like daydreams) or those that turn out, contrary to appearance, to be constructions (like screen memories); fantasies are also an outcome of psychoanalysis, an end result, a latent content to be revealed behind the symptom. Thus, from being a *mnemic symbol* of trauma, the symptom becomes a *staging of fantasies*[34] (e.g., a fantasy of prostitution, of "street walking," could be found behind the symptom of agoraphobia).

Freud begins to explore the domain of these fantasies by making an inventory, by describing the most typical forms. Seen at once from two sides, as manifest fact and as latent content, at the intersection of two paths approaching it from opposite directions, fantasy acquires the consistency of an object, the specific object of psychoanalysis. From here on, analysis will live with fantasy as "psychic reality," exploring its variations and, above all, analyzing its process and structure. Between 1897 and 1906 Freud published all the great works that reveal the mechanisms of the unconscious, that is to say, the transformations (in the sense in which the term is used in geometry) of fantasy: *The Interpretation of Dreams, The Psychopathology of Everyday Life, Jokes and Their Relation to the Unconscious.*

But, and this is our third current, in the trajectory of Freud's research and of his psychoanalytic treatment there was, from the beginning, a regressive tendency toward origins, toward the foundation of the symptom and the organization of neurotic character. To see fantasy as an autonomous, stable domain to be explored is to leave aside the question of its origin, not only the origin of its structure, but the origin of its contents down to the most concrete detail. In this sense, nothing has changed, and the chronological quest, going back in time to the first, real, verifiable *elements,* continues to orient Freud's practice.

In 1899, speaking of one of his patients, he writes: "Buried deep beneath all his fantasies, we found a scene from his primal period (before twenty-two months) which meets all the requirements and in which all the remaining puzzles converge."[35] And a little later, these lines in which he confesses the consuming passion to pursue his investigations ever further, confident of ending up—

---

34 Translator's note: "mise en scène de fantasmes."
35 Letter of December 21, 1899, *Complete Letters,* p. 391.

using a third party if necessary—by confirming the correctness of his investigation: *"In the evenings I read prehistory and the like, without any serious purpose. . . .*[36] In E's case, the second genuine scene is coming up after years of preparation; and it is one which may *perhaps* be confirmed objectively by asking his elder sister. Behind it, a third, long-suspected scene approaches."[37]

Freud calls these scenes from the earliest period, these *true* scenes, *Urszenen* ("primal" or "primitive" scenes). Later, as we know, this term will be limited to the child's observation of parental coitus. Refer to Freud's discussion in the Wolf Man case[38] of the relationship between the pathogenic dream and the primal scene on which it was based. Reading the first version of the clinical work, written in "the winter of 1914/15 shortly after the end of the treatment," one is struck by the passionate conviction that drives Freud, like a detective on the trail, to establish the reality of the scene by reconstructing it in detail. If such a concern can be present so long after "abandonment" of the seduction theory, isn't it proof that Freud never resigned himself to putting the "scenes" in the same category as *purely* imaginative creations? The question about the scene of seduction, strangulated twenty years earlier, returns in identical terms for the parental coitus observed by the Wolf Man. In Freud's thinking, the fundamental schema that underpins the seduction theory was not made obsolete by the discovery of infantile sexuality: he continues to invoke the same process of production *après-coup*.[39] With the Wolf Man, we rediscover the two events (here the scene and the dream) separated in

---

36 Emphasis ours.

37 Freud to Fliess, January 8, 1900, *Complete Letters*, p. 395.

38 "From the History of an Infantile Neurosis" (1918 [1914]), *Standard Edition* XVII, pp. 7–122.

39 Translator's note: The problem of translating *Nachträglichkeit* has not had a happy solution in English. Usually it has been rendered by the misleading, one-sided *deferred action* or by the equally one-sided *retrospective modification*. Laplanche suggested "afterwardsness" (see 'Notes on Afterwardsness'). In the UIT series we have decided to use *après-coup*, which has by now become common in English.

time, the first remaining not understood, excluded within the subject, and waiting to be elaborated at a later time. That this whole process is shifted to the years of infancy changes nothing essential in the theoretical model.

There is an evident resemblance between the Freudian schema of *après-coup* (*Nachträglichkeit*) and the psychotic mechanism of *foreclosure* unpacked by Lacan: whatever is not admitted to the symbolic order, which is "foreclosed" or "repudiated," reappears in the real in the form of an hallucination. But this nonsymbolization is precisely the first stage described by Freud. As Lacan and Freud both use the case of the Wolf Man to illustrate their theories, one could ask if Lacan didn't see as a psychotic symptom what is, in reality, a very general process, or ask, inversely, if Freud didn't take the exception for the rule, basing his demonstration on a case that turns out to be one of psychosis.

As it happens, Freud's argument is strengthened by the probable *reality* of the primal scene in this case. But one could imagine that the absence of subjective elaboration or of symbolization, a characteristic of the first stage, is a privilege limited to scenes actually lived. This "foreign body," which will be encysted within the subject, is generally brought to the subject not by the perception of a scene but rather by parental desire and the fantasies that undergird it. This would be typical of neurosis: in a first stage—a time that, because it is fragmented in a series of moments of autoerotism, cannot be situated precisely (see below)—a "pre-symbolic symbolic" (to paraphrase Freud) is created and isolated within the subject. In the second stage it is taken up *après-coup* and symbolized by the subject. In psychosis, in the first stage it would be raw reality that is imposed, evidently not symbolized by the subject, and having an irreducible nucleus resistant to all subsequent attempts at symbolization. That explains the catastrophic character of the failure of the second stage in psychoses.

This approach shows the distinction between primal repression and the psychotic mechanism that Freud tried to mark out throughout his work—particularly by calling the latter *Verleugnung*, denial (which Lacan called foreclosure).

It is well known that, in 1917, before publishing the Wolf Man manuscript, Freud added two long discussions that show he had been shaken by Jung's theory of "retrospective fantasy" (*Zurückphantasieren*). He admits that since the analysis results in a reconstruction, the scene could well have been constructed by the subject himself, but he insists nonetheless that perception supplied significant elements, even if only the sight of dogs copulating.

But most important, at the very moment Freud seems about to give up the prospect of getting support from the *ground of reality*—which on investigation crumbles away—he introduces a new notion, that of *Urphantasien*, primal fantasies.[40] Here we are present for a real mutation of the need for a theoretical foundation: because it is clearly impossible to determine if this primal "scene" is a lived event or a fiction. It is necessary to find a new foundation for fantasy, one that transcends both the individual's lived experience and his fantasy.

For us too, it is only *après-coup* that the meaning of the change in Freud's thinking in 1897 becomes clear. Seemingly nothing has changed: the same search for a truly *first* scene continues; the same schema is present, a dialectic between two successive historical events and—as if Freud had learned nothing—the same disappointment at the escape of an ultimate event, of a first scene. But in what we have called the second current, the discovery of the unconscious as a structured domain that can be reconstructed because it is itself an arrangement of elements decomposed and recomposed according to certain laws, we have a domain that will permit the search for origins to unfold in a new dimension.

---

40 *Urszene, Urphantasie*: the words have the same prefix, *Ur*. It is found in other Freudian terms, notably *Urverdrängung* (primal or primary repression).

The concept of primal fantasies[41] merges what one can call Freud's desire to find the bedrock of the event (if it disappears in the history of the individual as a consequence of being refracted and reduced, one goes back ever further...) and the need to base the structure of fantasy on something other than the event.

Ur

Primal fantasies constitute "the treasure-trove of unconscious fantasies of all neurotics, and probably of all human beings."[42] These words alone suggest that it is not only the empirical fact of their frequency, even their ubiquity, that distinguishes them. If "the same phantasies with the same content are created on every occasion,"[43] if we can find several "typical"[44] fantasies within the diversity of personal narratives, it is because the individual's factual history is not the *prime mover* and it is necessary to posit a preexisting schema capable of serving as an "organizer."

Freud saw only one possibility to account for such antecedence: a phylogenetic explanation. "It seems to me quite possible that all the things that are told to us to-day in analysis as phantasy— the seduction of children, the inflaming of sexual excitement by observing parental intercourse, the threat of castration (or rather castration itself)—were once real occurrences in the primaeval times of

---

41 When we speak of the *concept* we could be accused of the sin of excess. It is true that "primal fantasy" is not part of the classical conceptual apparatus of psychoanalysis. Freud invokes it only in the context of the issue whose development we have tried to unpack. The phrase, thus, has the value of a sign, and by this fact calls out for interpretation.

42 "A Case of Paranoia Running Counter to the Psychoanalytic Theory of the Disease" (1915), *Standard Edition* XIV, p. 269.

43 *Introductory Lectures, Standard Edition* XVI, p. 370.

44 A concern of Freud's from very early on. See Draft M: "There is the soundest hope that it will be possible to determine the number and kind of fantasies just as it is possible with scenes." *Complete Letters*, p. 248.

the human family, and that children in their phantasies are simply filling in the gaps in individual truth with prehistoric truth."[45] So once again a "real" is postulated behind the elaborations of fantasy, but, as Freud emphasizes, it is a "real" that has an autonomous and structuralizing relation to subjects who are completely dependent on it. He goes quite far in this direction, admitting the possibility of a difference between the "schema" and individual experiences that can shape psychic conflict.[46]

It is tempting to see this "real" that shapes the play of imagination and imposes its law on it as an anticipation of "symbolic order" as defined by Levi-Strauss and Lacan, showing its organization and its power in both ethnology and psychoanalysis. *Totem and Taboo* claims to recount the framework of these scenes that go back to the prehistory of man, and that are attributed to primal man (*Urmensch*) and to the primal father (*Urvater*). Freud invoked them less to recover a reality that had escaped him on the level of individual history than to restrict the imaginary, which otherwise would lack an organizing principle and thus would not constitute "the nucleus of the unconscious."

Under the pseudoscientific mask of phylogenesis, in the appeal to *inherited memory traces*, we should recognize Freud's conceptual need to postulate a meaningful organization prior to the action of the event and prior to all of the signified. In this mythical prehistory of the species there is the need for a prestructure inaccessible to the subject, beyond his initiatives and decisions, outside his inner "kitchen" (however rich the ingredients our new sorcerers can conjure up). But Freud

---

45 *Introductory Lectures, Standard Edition* XVI, p. 371.

46 "Wherever experiences fail to fit in with the hereditary schema, they become remodeled in the imagination. ... It is precisely such cases that are calculated to convince us of the independent existence of the schema. We are often able to see the schema triumphing over the experience of the individual; as when in our present case the boy's father became the castrator and the menace of his infantile sexuality in spite of what was in other respects an inverted Oedipus complex. . . . The contradictions between experience and the schema seem to supply the conflicts of childhood with an abundance of material." In the *History of an Infantile Neurosis, Standard Edition* XVII, pp. 119–120.

is literally trapped by his own concepts. Even in this false synthesis in which the past of the human species is preserved in hereditary schemas, he reencounters the opposition he vainly sought to transcend: the opposition between events and constitution.

Okay. But let's not rush to replace this "phylogenetic explanation" with an interpretation along structuralist lines. Apart from the subject's history but nonetheless within history, a discourse and symbolic chain but permeated with the imaginary, a structure but activated by contingent elements, primal fantasy is first of all a fantasy and as such is marked by traits making it difficult to assimilate into a purely transcendental scheme, even if it furnishes lived experience with the conditions of possibility.

Here we do not claim to give an account of the relation between the level of oedipal structure and that of primal fantasies, which a coherent psychoanalytic theory would require. It would first be necessary to specify how oedipal structure is to be understood. It should be noted that the structural aspect of the Oedipus complex— considered both in its inaugural function and in its triangular form—was unpacked by Freud only quite late in his work; for example, it is completely absent in *Three Essays* (1905). What is called the complete Oedipus only appears in *The Ego and the Id* (1923), and the "completeness" in question cannot be understood in a formalist sense: it points to a limited series of concrete positions within the interpsychological domain created by the father-mother-child triangle. From the perspective of structural anthropology, one can detect here one modality of the law governing exchange between humans, a law susceptible, in other cultures, of being incarnated in other persons and other forms. For instance, the prohibitive function of the law could be embodied in someone other than the father. If, as psychoanalysts, we accept this solution, we would lose a fundamental dimension of our experience: the subject is indeed put into a structure of exchange, but the structure is transmitted to him by the unconscious of the parents, and thus is less assimilable to a language system than to the particular details of speech.

In fact, Freud's conceptualization of Oedipus is marked by realism: whether represented as an internal conflict—"the nuclear conflict"—or as a social institution, the complex remains a given that the subject *encounters*: "Every new arrival on this planet is faced by the task of mastering the Oedipus complex . . ."[47]

Maybe it was this realist conception that allowed Freud to permit the coexistence of the Oedipus complex and the concept of primal fantasies without being concerned about how they fit together. With primal fantasy, the subject doesn't encounter structure; rather, the subject is carried by primal fantasy (let us repeat the point) to the interior of the fantasy, to knowledge of a configuration of unconscious desires, and not as a combinatorial term.

The text in which Freud mentions *Urphantasien* for the first time leaves no doubt about this.[48] It takes up the case of a paranoid woman who maintained she had been observed and photographed while lying next to her lover; she had heard "a noise," the click of a camera. Behind this delusion, Freud finds the primal scene: the noise is the noise of parents who wake up the child; it is also the noise the child is afraid to make lest it betray her listening. How can we understand the role of the noise in the fantasy? In one sense, Freud says, it is merely a "provoking factor," an "accidental" cause; it only "activated the typical fantasy of eavesdropping which is part of the parental complex." But he immediately corrects himself: "Indeed, it is doubtful whether we can rightly call the noise 'accidental'. . . such noises are on the contrary an indispensable part of the fantasy of eavesdropping."[49] Indeed, the noise invoked by the patient[50] reproduces, in the present,

---

47 *Three Essays, Standard Edition* VII, p. 226 n (footnote added in 1920).
48 "A Case of Paranoia" (1915), *Standard Edition* XIV.
49 *Ibid.*, p. 269 [*Standard Edition* translation modified].
50 The noise, according to Freud, is a projection. A pulsation in the clitoris transformed and projected as a noise. The pulsation of the drive (*la pulsation de la pulsion*) would be a play on words evoking a new circular relationship between the pulsation that actualizes the fantasy and the drive that arouses it.

the sign of the primal fantasy, the element from which all subsequent elaboration of fantasy can begin. In other words, *the origin of the fantasy is integrated into the very structure of the primal fantasy.*

In his first theoretical sketches stimulated by the question of fantasy, Freud emphasizes the role of hearing in a way that may intrigue his readers.[51] Without giving too much weight to these fragmentary texts in which Freud seems for the most part to have paranoid fantasies in mind, one must still ask why he privileges hearing. In our opinion, there are two reasons. One involves the *perceptual system* involved: at the moment something is heard, it ruptures the continuity of an undifferentiated perceptual field; at the same time, it creates a sign (the noise anticipated and perceived in the night), putting the subject in the position of having to respond. To that degree, the prototype of the signifier belongs to the heard, even if it finds similarities in other sensory modalities. But—and this is the second reason Freud explicitly mentions in the passage in question—what is heard is also the history, or the legends, of parents, of grandparents, of ancestors: the family sayings and rumors, that spoken or secret discourse existing prior to the subject, in which he arrives and must find his way. To the extent that it retroactively summons up the discourse, the noise, like any other discrete sensory element that can function as an index, will take on the meaning of that discourse.

In their very content, in their *themes* (primal scene, castration, seduction), primal fantasies also point toward a retroactive presumption: *they go back to origins.* Like myths, they seem to bring a picture and a "solution" to what the child sees as major enigmas; they dramatize as moments of emergence, as the beginning of a story, what the subject

---

51 "They are made up of things that are *heard*, and made use of *subsequently*; thus they combine things that have been experienced and things that have been heard, past events (from the history of parents and ancestors) and things that have been seen by oneself. They are related to things heard, as dreams are related to things seen." Draft L, *Standard Edition* I, p. 248; and also, "Fantasies arise from an unconscious combination . . . of things experienced and heard." Draft M, *Standard Edition* I, p. 252.

sees as a reality whose nature demands an explanation, a "theory."

Fantasies of origins: in the primal scene, it is the origin of the individual that is depicted; in fantasies of seduction, it is the origin of, the arousal of, sexuality; in fantasies of castration, it is the origin of sexual difference. Thus one finds in each theme, doubly signified, the "already there" quality of primal fantasies.

Convergence of theme, of structure, and probably of function: in the indication provided by the perceptual domain, in the constructed scenario, in the search for beginnings, what appears on the stage of fantasy is that which "originates" the subject himself.

(If we ask ourselves what these fantasies mean *for us,* we would start at another level of interpretation. They are not only part of the symbolic order, but, through the mediation of an imaginary scenario, they translate the insertion of the most radically inaugural symbolic into the reality of the body. For us, what does the primal scene represent? The conjunction between the biological fact of conception (and of birth) and the symbolic fact of filiation, the conjunction between the "savage act" of coitus and the existence of the mother-child-father triad. In fantasies of castration the conjunction of the real and the symbolic is even more evident. As for seduction, we believe we have shown, Freud could theorize fantasy not only because he came upon many real cases of seduction—discovering by this detour the function of fantasy—but also because he tried to understand, in terms of origins, the way in which sexuality comes to the human being.)

A scenario with multiple entries

Found at the most diverse levels of psychoanalytic experience—fact, interpretation, reconstruction, hypothesis, fantasy necessarily presents the difficult problem of its metapsychological status, first of all the question of its location in a model of mind that distinguishes between the systems unconscious, preconscious, and conscious.

In a certain trend within contemporary psychoanalysis there has been an attempt to settle the question by transposing into theory a distinction that seems clinically necessary between the fantasies offered up for interpretation and the fantasy that is the end result of psychoanalytic interpretation.[52] From this point of view, Freud was wrong to use one term, *Phantasie,* for two completely distinct realities: on the one hand unconscious Phantasie, "the primary content of unconscious mental processes,"[53] and, on the other, conscious or sublimated imaginings whose prototype is the daydream. The latter is but a manifest content, like any other; it has no more of a privileged relationship with unconscious *Phantasie* than do dreams or behavior or what in general we call "material": like all manifest data, they would be interpreted in terms of unconscious *Phantasie.* To get rid of this unhappy confusion, these colleagues propose different spellings to distinguish conscious "fantasies" like daydreams from unconscious "phantasies." Does this constitute, as is sometimes claimed, great progress, the result of half a century of psychoanalysis? Let us try to compare this "progress" to the *inspiration* and *progression* of Freudian thought.

The inspiration of Freud's thought: by stubbornly using the same term, *Phantasie,* to the very end of his work, in spite of the very early discovery that these *Phantasien* could be unconscious as well as conscious, Freud wants to demonstrate a deep relationship: "The contents of the clearly conscious fantasies of perverts (which in favorable circumstances can be transformed into manifest behavior), of the delusional fears of paranoiac's (which are projected in a hostile sense onto other people) and of the unconscious fantasies of hysterics (which psychoanalysis reveals behind their symptoms)—all of these coincide with one another even down to their details."[54] This is to say

---

52 See especially Susan Isaacs, "The Nature and Function of Phantasy," (1954) *International Journal of Psychoanalysis* 29: pp. 73–97.
53 *Ibid.,* p. 81.
54 *Three Essays on Sexuality, Standard Edition* VII, pp. 165–166 n.

that in imaginative formations and in psychopathological structures
as diverse as those Freud mentions in this passage, the same content, the same arrangement, can be found, whether it is conscious or
unconscious, acted out or represented, and whether or not there has
been a change of sign or permutation of person.

Such an affirmation, coming in 1905, is not from a "proto-
Freud." It is central, notably from 1906–1909, when fantasy was the
subject of much of his research.[55] In this period, the power of unconscious fantasy is plainly recognized (e.g., as underlying the hysterical
attack that symbolizes the fantasy). Nevertheless, Freud begins with
conscious fantasy, with daydreams, not only as paradigm but as
source. These hysterical fantasies, which "have important connec-
tions with the causation of the neurotic symptoms" (doesn't this refer
to unconscious fantasies) have as "a common source and normal
prototype . . . what are called the day-dreams of youth."[56] "A common source"? Indeed, conscious fantasy itself can be repressed and
so become pathogenic. It is in fantasy that Freud finds the privileged
point at which one can see *in vivo* the process of passing from one
system to another: repression or the return of the repressed.[57] It is
clearly the same mixed entity, the same "mixed blood" that, close to
the boundary of the unconscious, can pass from one side to the other

55 "Gradiva" (1907), "Creative Writers and Daydreaming" (1908), "Hysterical Fantasies and Their Relation to Bisexuality" (1908), "Some General Remarks on Hysterical
Attacks" (1909), "Family Romances (1909).
56 "Hysterical Phantasies and Their Relation to Bisexuality," *Standard Edition* IX, p.
159.
57 "In favourable circumstances, the subject can still capture an unconscious
phantasy of this sort in consciousness. After I had drawn the attention of one of
my patients to her phantasies, she told me that on one occasion she had suddenly
found herself in tears in the street and that, rapidly considering what it was she was
actually crying about, she had got hold of a phantasy to the following effect. In her
imagination she had formed at tender attachment to a pianist who was well known
in town (though she was not personally acquainted with him); she had had a child
by him (she was in fact childless); and he had then deserted her and her child and
left them in poverty. It was at this point in her romance that she had burst into tears."
Ibid., p. 160.

largely as a function of the degree of investment.[58] One might object that in such passages Freud is not dealing with unconscious fantasy at the deepest level, that he is not grappling with "phantasy" but with a simple, sublimated daydream. However, Freud clearly uses the word *repression* to designate the process that "thrusts back" the fantasy, and he calls the boundary he is speaking of the unconscious in the precise, topographic sense.

We certainly don't deny that there are different levels of unconscious fantasies, but it is striking that when Freud studies the metapsychology of dreams he finds the same relationship between the deepest unconscious fantasies and daydreams: in the dream work fantasy is present at both ends of the process. At one end, it is linked to the deepest unconscious desire, the "capitalist" of the dream, and in that role it is at the origin of the "zigzag journey" that the excitation is supposed to travel across a succession of psychic systems: "The first portion [of the zigzag journey] was a progressive one, leading from the unconscious scenes or phantasies to the preconscious,"[59] where it recruits the "day's residues" or "transference thoughts." But fantasy is present also at the other end of the dream, in the secondary revision that Freud clearly emphasizes is not part of the dream work but must be identified "with the work of our waking thought." The secondary revision is a reworking a posteriori that, moreover, goes on after we have woken up in transformations we make to the dream's narrative. It consists essentially in adding a minimum of order and coherence to the raw product delivered by the unconscious mechanisms (displacement, condensation, and symbolization), in plating this irregular heap with a "façade," with a scenario that makes it relatively coherent and continuous. In a word, it makes the dream's final version look some-

---

58 "They draw near to consciousness and remain undisturbed so long as they do not have an intense cathexis, but as soon as they exceed a certain height of cathexis they are thrust back." In "The Unconscious," *Standard Edition* XIV, p. 191.
59 *Interpretation of Dreams, Standard Edition* V, p. 574.

thing like a "daydream."⁶⁰ In addition, secondary revision uses those fully formed scenarios, the fantasies or daydreams the subject created for himself during the day before the dream.

Does this mean there is *no* privileged relationship between the "phantasy" that is at the heart of the dream and the "fantasy" that helps to make it acceptable to the system Conscious? Full of his discovery that the dream is the fulfillment of an unconscious desire, it is understandable that Freud devalued everything that, close to consciousness, could appear as defense or as camouflage, including secondary revision.⁶¹ But he quickly returns to a different understanding: "It would be a mistake, however, to suppose that these dream-façades are nothing other than mistaken and somewhat arbitrary revisions of the dream-content by the conscious agency of our mental life.... The wishful phantasies revealed by analysis in night-dreams often turn out to be repetitions or modified versions of scenes from infancy; thus in some cases the façade of the dream directly reveals the dream's actual nucleus, distorted by an admixture of other material."⁶² Thus the two ends of the dream, and the two modes of fantasy that are found there, seem, if not to merge with each other, at least to have an internal communication and to symbolize each other.

We have spoken of a *progression* in Freud's thinking about the

---

60 *Ibid.*, pp. 490–491.

61 Of course one must undo the effect of the secondary revision in order to take up the dream element by element. But Freud does not forget that in *putting everything on the same level*—which is one aspect of analytic listening —the narrative structure, the scenario itself, becomes an element, exactly like, for example, the overall reaction of the subject to his own dream.

62 "On Dreams," *Standard Edition* V, p. 667. In a general fashion, Freud also seems to indicate that desire can be more easily read in the structure of a fantasy than in the structure of a dream (unless the dream has been powerfully structured by the fantasy, as is especially true of "typical dreams": "If we examine their structure [fantasies], we shall perceive the way in which the wishful purpose that is at work in their production has mixed up the material of which they are built, has re-arranged it and has formed it into a new whole." *Interpretation of Dreams, Standard Edition* V, p. 492.

metapsychological status of fantasy. His thinking certainly moves in the direction of differentiation but, as we believe we have demonstrated, without suppressing the homology that exists between different levels of fantasy and, above all, without making the major line of differentiation coincide with the topographic barrier (the censorship) that separates the preconscious-conscious on one side from the unconscious on the other. The differentiation occurs within the unconscious: "Unconscious phantasies either have been unconscious all along and have been formed in the unconscious; or—as is more often the case—they were once conscious phantasies, day-dreams, and have since been purposely forgotten and have become unconscious through 'repression'."[63]

A little later, this distinction will coincide in Freud's terminology with the distinction between primal fantasies and other fantasies—unconscious or not—which could be called secondary fantasies.[64]

Beyond this fundamental difference, the unity of fantasy as a whole resides in their having the character of mixed entities in which the structural and the imaginary are found, granted in varying proportion. It is in this sense that as his model of fantasy Freud always

---

63 "Hysterical Phantasies and Their Relation to Bisexuality," *Standard Edition* IX, p. 161.
64 We propose the following table:

Urphantasie	Phantasie (secondary)	
(unconscious original)	unconscious $\leftarrow$	$\rightarrow$ conscious
	(repressed)	(day-dream)

The repression that "returns" secondary fantasies into the unconscious would be what Freud calls "secondary repression" or "after-pressure" (*refoulement après-coup*). The formation or the inscription of primal fantasies within the individual corresponds to another type of repression, more obscure and more mythical, that Freud calls "primal repression" (*Urverdrängung*). Below we try to point out an approach to this. See also J. Laplanche and S. Leclaire, L'Inconscient: Une étude psychanalytique," *Les Temps Modernes*, July 1961.

uses the daydream, that dime novel, both stereotypic and infinitely variable, that the subject creates and recounts to himself while awake.

Play of images: both daydreams, using the colorful hodge-podge of individual experience, and primal fantasy, whose dramatis personae, the face cards of the deck, get their regalia from a family legend mutilated, turned upside down, and misunderstood. Structure: primal fantasy, in which it is easy to read the oedipal configuration, and also daydreams, as analysis reveals typical, repetitive scenarios under the variability of these confabulations.

Nevertheless, it is not only—nor even essentially—the variable and inverse proportion of imaginary ingredients to binding structure that permits classification and differentiation of the modes of fantasy[65] into a spectrum between the poles of primal fantasy and daydream. The structure itself seems to vary. At the daydream pole, the scenario is essentially in the first person: the place of the subject is clear and invariable. The organization is stabilized by secondary process and by the "ego": the subject, it is said, *lives* his dream. On the contrary, at the other pole, primal fantasy is characterized by an absence of subjectivization going hand and hand with the presence of the subject *in* the scene. For example, the child is one of the characters, among others, in the fantasy "a child is being beaten." In this sense, primal fantasy has a close relation to screen memory, for which Freud laid particular stress on this visualization of the subject at the same level as the other protagonists.[66]

"A father seduces a daughter," for example, is the summary formulation of the fantasy of seduction. Here the mark of primary process is not in the absence of organization, but the peculiar character of the structure: it is a scenario with multiple entries; nothing

---

65 In which number one must include both screen memories and the sexual theories of children.

66 This aspect of screen memories is, for Freud, proof that they are not true memories. Yet among conscious fantasies, they are the only ones which present themselves as reality. True scenes, they are the screens for scenes or for primal fantasies.

indicates that at the beginning the subject finds her place in the word *daughter;* it could equally well be in the word *father* or even the word *seduces.*

The moment of "auto": origin of sexuality

When Freud asks himself whether there is anything in human beings comparable to "instinct in animals,"[67] he finds an equivalence not in drives (*Triebe*) but precisely in primal fantasies.[68] A precious clue, first in that it provides an indirect proof of a repugnance to finding the solution to the problem of fantasy in a biological hypothesis: far from trying to base fantasy on the drives, Freud would rather make the play of drives depend on antecedent fantasy structures. It is precious also because it helps situate certain contemporary conceptions. Finally, it leads us to wondering about the tight relation, embedded in the term *Wunschphantasie*, between fantasy and desire.

Susan Isaacs, for example, says primal fantasies are "an activity parallel to drives from which they emerge." In them she sees the "psychic expression" of experience itself defined by the field of forces created by the drives—libidinal and aggressive—and the defenses they provoke. Finally she wants to make a tight link between specific forms of fantasy life and bodily zones that are the seat of the drives. Isn't this how she is led to misunderstand Freud's contributions concerning both drive and fantasy? For her, fantasy is only the imaginary transcription of each drive's basic aim, an aim that from the very start has a specific object; "instinctual pressure" is necessarily experienced as a fantasy that, whatever its content (e.g., an infant's desire to suck),

---

67 The Unconscious, op. cit., p. 195
68 "History of an Infantile Neurosis," op. cit., p. 120.

once it can be verbalized[69] presents itself in the form of a "sentence" containing three elements: subject (I), verb (swallow, bite, reject), object (breast, mother).[70] Of course, because for the Kleinians drives are intrinsically a *relation,* Isaacs shows how a fantasy like incorporation is also experienced as being incorporated, the active becoming passive; what's more, this fear of a "return to sender" is constitutive of fantasy itself. But is it sufficient to recognize in the fantasy of incorporation the equivalence of eating and being eaten? If we maintain the idea that the subject has a place, even in a passive role, are we at the deepest level of fantasy?

If, for Isaacs, fantasy constitutes an immediate expression of drive, almost consubstantial with it, and if in the last instance fantasy can be reduced to the relation that links a subject and an object by a verb indicating an action (with the form of an omnipotent wish), it is because for her the structure of the drive is an intentionality inseparable from its aim: the drive intuits, "knows," the object that will satisfy it. Just as the fantasy, which at first expresses libidinal and aggressive drives, quickly morphs into a form of defense, in the end all the subject's internal dynamics are deployed along the lines of this unique organization. Such a conception postulates, in accord with certain Freudian formulations, that "all that is conscious has had a preliminary unconscious stage" and that "the ego is a differentiated

69 For Isaacs, "primary phantasies are . . . dealt with by mental processes far removed from words." It is only "to be able to speak of them" that we express them in words, but by doing so we introduce a "foreign element." Using one of Freud's formulations, Isaacs speaks of "the language of the drives"; and it is certainly true that it is not the verbal or nonverbal character that defines the nature of language. But if Isaacs confounds language and the power of expression, perhaps she misses what is most original in the conceptions of Melanie Klein: the attempt to grasp a language that is not made up of words but is nonetheless structured by paired opposites (good/bad, inside/outside). The technical audacity of Klein presupposes a reference not to the mobile expression of instinctual life, but to a few fundamental signifiers.
70 See the diverse variations formulated by Isaacs: "*I* want to eat her all up," "*I* want to keep her inside me," "*I* want to tear her to bits," "*I* want to throw her out of me," "*I* want to bring her back," "*I* must have her now," etc.

part of the id." This forces us to see an underlying fantasy in every mental operation, a fantasy that itself is in principle reducible to the aim of a drive. The biological subject is thus in direct continuity with the subject of the fantasy—the sexual, human subject—according to the sequence:

soma → id → fantasy (of desire, of defense) → ego mechanism

The action of repression must be badly understood, because "fantasy life" is implicit rather than repressed and because it contains in itself its own specific conflicts simply fantasies with contradictory aims coexist within the mind. In fact, one finds there a "profusion" of fantasy in which one cannot recognize the distinctive structure that Freud tried to reveal, a structure in which the relationship he established between fantasy and sexuality dissolves—a natural relationship although difficult to specify.

It is astonishing that, even after he had fully recognized the existence and extent of childhood sexual life and childhood fantasies—for instance in a note added to *Three Essays*[71] in 1920—Freud continued to connect fantasizing activity largely to the period of pubertal and to prepubertal masturbation.[72] Isn't it because in his eyes there is a close correlation between fantasy and autoerotism, a correlation not explained simply by the idea that autoerotism is disguised by fantasy?

Isn't he then simply sharing the common notion that, in the absence of a real object, the subject searches for and creates an imaginary satisfaction?

---

71 *Three Essays*, op. cit., p. 226.
72 Of course, masturbation usually implies an imaginary relation with an object; so it only from an external point of view that it can be called autoerotic. But an infantile autoerotic activity, thumb sucking for example, in no way implies the absence of an object. What essentially defines it as autoerotic is, as we explain below, a particular mode of satisfaction, specific to the birth of sexuality and of which something persists in pubertal masturbation.

When creating a theoretical model for the formation of desire's object and aim,[73] Freud himself endorsed this way of seeing things. The origin of fantasy lies in hallucinatory satisfaction of desire: the nursling, in the absence of the real object, reproduces as an hallucination the original experience of satisfaction. In this sense, the most fundamental fantasies would be those that tend refind the hallucinated objects linked to the earliest experience of the rise and satisfaction of desire.[74]

But even before disentangling what this Freudian fiction is supposed to explain, it is necessary to question its meaning, especially since, though it is rarely formulated in detail, it is always presumed by Freud in his conception of primary process. One could see it as a myth of origin: what Freud claims to have recaptured, and that he gives a figurative representation, is the moment at which desire emerges. This is an analytic "construction," or fantasy, that tries to get at that moment of cleavage of *before* and *after* that still contains both: the mythical moment of disjunction between the appeasement of need (*Befriedigung*) and the fulfillment of desire (*Wunscherfüllung*), between the time of real experience and the time of its hallucinatory

---

73 "The first wishing seems to have been a hallucinatory cathecting of the memory of satisfaction" In *Interpretation of Dreams, Standard Edition* V, p. 598.

74 See, e.g., Isaacs's interpretation of Freud's hypothesis of the first hallucination: "It seems probable that hallucination works best at times of less intense instinctual tension, perhaps when the infant half-awakes and first begins to be hungry. . . . The pain of frustration then stirs up a still stronger desire, viz. the wish to take the whole breast into himself and keep it there, as a source of satisfaction; and this in its turn will for a time omnipotently fulfil itself in belief, in hallucination. . . . This hallucination of the internal satisfying breast may, however, break down altogether if frustration continues and hunger is not satisfied, instinct- tension proving too strong to be denied." "The Nature and Function of Phantasy," *International Journal of Psychoanalysis* 29, p. 81.

It is easy to see the embarrassing difficulty Isaacs has trying to reconcile the idea of an hallucinatory *satisfaction* with the demands of a frustrated instinct. How can an infant "feed" itself on the wind? This Freudian model becomes incomprehensible unless one understands that the "primal hallucination" is not of the real object but of the lost object, not the milk but the breast that signifies it.

revival, between the object that gratifies and the sign[75] that simultaneously marks the object and its absence. The mythical moment of the rejoining of hunger and sexuality at their point of origin.

If we ourselves, caught in the fantasy of origins, now claim to have found the origin of fantasy—this time placing it in the course of the real history of the child, in the development of sexuality (the perspective of the second chapter of *Three Essays*)—we reconnect it to the appearance of autoerotism: the moment when, in the world of needs, the "vital" functions whose goals and mechanisms are fixed and whose objects are preformed, detach themselves—not as the pleasure found in satisfying a function (of whatever kind), not as the pleasure of reducing the tension that created the need, but as a marginal product that Freud calls the "pleasure premium."

But in speaking of the appearance of autoerotism, even though we avoid turning it into a stage of development of the libido, even though we underline its permanence and presence in all adult sexual behavior, we risk overlooking the very meaning of the notion and what it can demonstrate about both the *function* and the *structure* of fantasy.

If the notion of autoerotism is often criticized in psychoanalytic writing, it is because it is misunderstood to be a category of object relations, considered as a first stage, enclosed within itself, from which the subject must rejoin the world of objects. It is easy, using a tremendous amount of observational data, to confront this account with the variety and complexity of the links that, from the beginning, unite the infant and the external object, most importantly the mother. When Freud speaks of autoerotism, principally in *Three Essays*, he has no intention of denying the existence of a primary relation with the object; on the contrary, he clearly indicates that the drive *becomes* autoerotic only after having lost its object.[76]

---

75 The breast, which psychoanalysts have named in error the "object of desire."
76 Translator's note: Laplanche and Pontalis put the remainder of this paragraph in a footnote.

> At a time at which the first beginnings of sexual satisfac-
> tion are still linked with the taking of nourishment, the
> sexual drive has a sexual object outside the infant's own
> body in the shape of his mother's breast. *It is only later*
> *that the drive loses that object, just at the time, perhaps, when*
> *the child is able to form a total idea of the person to whom the*
> *organ that is giving him satisfaction belongs.* As a rule the
> sexual drive then becomes auto-erotic..."[77]

A precious passage also because of the hint in contains (in the words we have italicized): in its formation the autoerotic fantasy contains not only the part object (breast, thumb taken as substitute) but the mother as a whole person who thus withdraws at the very moment of her totalization. This "totalization" should not be understood on the level of a perceptual gestalt, but in terms of the infant's demand, which the mother grants or denies.[78]

If one can say of autoerotism that it is objectless (*objektlos*), it is in no sense because it appears before all relations with an object,[79] nor because with the arrival of autoerotism objects are no longer sought out for satisfaction, but only because the natural mode of apprehending the object is split: the sexual drive separates from the nonsexual functions (alimentary, for example) on which it leans[80] and from which it takes its aim and object.

Thus, the "origin" of autoerotism is the moment in which sexuality detaches itself from any natural object, gives itself over to fantasy, and by that very process creates itself as sexuality. This

---

77 Three Essays, *Standard Edition* VII, p. 222.

78 Translator's note: I.e., the mother as a whole object capable of good or bad, satisfying or frustrating intentions / acts.

79 Some analysts call this an "objectless stage" in a genetic conception that one could call totalitarian because it confuses the formation of the libidinal object with that of objectivity in the external world and t claims to establish stages in the development of the ego as an "organ of reality"; they claim as well that these stages are correlated with the stages of libidinal development.

80 Elsewhere we develop this notion, which is fundamental to the Freudian theory of the drives (*The Language of Psycho-analysis*).

moment is more abstract than located in time, both because it is constantly renewed and because it is necessary to assume the existence of an erotic excitation before it can be sought for as such. But, looked at in the opposite way, couldn't it be said that it is the irruption of fantasy that provokes this disjunction between sexuality and need?[81] Circular causality or simultaneous birth? The fact is that, however far back one goes, fantasy and sexuality find their origin at the same point.

Autoerotic satisfaction, to the extent that it exists in an autonomous state, is defined by a very precise trait: it is the product of the anarchic activity of partial drives strictly linked to the excitation of specified erogenous zones (an excitation that is born and satisfied in the same place); it is not the global pleasure of functioning, but rather a fragmented pleasure, an organ pleasure (*Organlust*) narrowly located.

The capacity for being erogenous is inherent in certain "predestined" bodily zones (thus, in the activity of sucking, the oral zone is predestined by its very physiology to acquire erotic value), but this potential exists in any organ (even internal organs), in any region with any bodily function. In all cases, the function serves only as support. For example, the ingestion of food serves as a model for the fantasy of incorporation. Modeled on the function, sexuality is precisely what is *different* from the function; in this sense, its prototype is not nursing but nonnutritive sucking, the moment when the external object is abandoned, when the aim and the source become autonomous from eating and the digestive system. One could almost say that the ideal form of autoerotism are "those lips which kiss themselves"[82]: in this enjoyment seemingly closed in on itself, as at the deepest level of

---

81 In one of his first reflections on fantasy, Freud notes that the impulses can emanate from fantasies. *Complete Letters*, p. 250.

82 See "Three Essays" and also "Instincts and Their Vicissitudes," in which Freud analyzes the paired opposites sadism/masochism and voyeurism/exhibitionism. Beneath the active or passive form (e.g., to see / to be seen), there must be a reflexive form (to see oneself) that according to Freud would be primordial. One must look for this primordial instance when the subject no longer situates himself in one of the terms of the fantasy.

fantasy, in a discourse addressed to no one, the distinction between subject and object is abolished.

Let us add that Freud constantly stressed the role of the mother (or others) as seducer when she washes, dresses, and caresses her child[83]; and, further, that the privileged erogenous zones (oral, anal, urogenital, skin) are at the same time the regions getting the most attention from the mother and that have a manifest signification of exchange (orifices or skin covering). Thus, it is clear how certain chosen locations of the body can serve not only to support a local pleasure but to provide a meeting place with desire, with maternal fantasy, and through that with a form of primal fantasy.

In situating the origin of fantasy in the *time* of autoerotism, we have marked the connection of fantasy with desire. But fantasy is not the object of desire; it is the staging of desire.[84] In fantasy, the subject does not pursue the object or its sign, but pictures himself involved in a sequence of images. He does not simply represent the desired object; rather, he represents himself as participating in the scene, though in the forms of fantasy closest to primal fantasy he cannot be assigned a specific place. (Hence the danger in clinical practice of interpretations that claim to do so.) Consequences: while always present in the fantasy, the subject may be represented in a desubjectivized form, which is to say, in the very syntax of the sequence in question. Also, to the extent that desire is not a pure arousal of drive, but is articulated in the fantasy's sentence, this fantasy sentence is the chosen site of the most primitive defensive mechanisms, including turning against the

---

83 "A child's intercourse with anyone responsible for his care affords him an unending source of sexual excitation and satisfaction from his erotogenic zones. This is especially so since the person in charge of him, who, after all, is as a rule his mother, herself regards him with feelings that are derived from her own sexual life: she strokes him, kisses him, rocks him and quite clearly treats him as a substitute for a complete sexual object." *Three Essays*, Standard Edition VII, p. 223.

Nevertheless, it is classically said that Freud took a long time to recognize the bond with the mother!

84 Translator's note: "Staging" in the sense that a play is staged (*la mise en scène du desire*).

self, reversal into the opposite, projection, and denial; these defenses are indissolubly linked to the primary function of fantasy—the staging of desire—inasmuch as desire itself is formed as a prohibition, inasmuch as the conflict is a *conflict at the origin, a primal conflict*.

As for knowing the director of this staging, psychoanalysts must not rely on the resources of our science, or even those of myth. We must become philosophers.

Preface to
Beyond the Pleasure Principle

by Jean Laplanche

Preface to
Beyond the Pleasure Principle

Here is a text that can be read dozens of times, in whole or in part—it is divided into chapters, each retaining a degree of autonomy of thought and style while remaining interwoven with the others. It would be a mistake to assume that the book's topic can be defined straightaway on the basis of its title. "Beyond" could indeed imply that Freud wants to go further than the pleasure principle, into a "beyond" that may be metaphysical. Yet the German preposition *jenseits* is itself as misleading as its translation; as we will see in the course of the text, what is at issue is neither a vision of the future nor, a fortiori, an eschatology, but something located "out there beyond" if not "below" the pleasure principle.

We will summarize book's seven chapters succinctly before uncovering a few general questions.

Chapter 1. Are there any truly inherent limitations in the functioning of the "pleasure principle"? In any case, Freud strives to reduce them by adopting what he calls an economic perspective; that is to say, he speaks of quantities of psychic energy circulating in the apparatus. Let us note that this energy is in no way specified according to the various types of drives involved: pleasure is envisioned as a correlative of any decrease in tension in the apparatus, unpleasure as an increase in this tension.

Freud also resorts to more technical notions such as homeostasis. The biological system would essentially be led by a tendency toward the stablest possible state, even to "zero," a complete absence of tension. In fact, one can raise many questions about Freud's formulations, such as the question, which he asks in passing, of what *unconscious* pleasure or unpleasure might be, something that is diffi-cult to envisage but that the theory of psychic conflict and symptoms nonetheless requires.

Chapter 2. In this chapter new limitations of the pleasure prin-ciple are related to traumatic or posttraumatic situations, as can be observed in accident-induced or war neuroses on the one hand (World War I had just ended when this text was written) and with less vio-lent traumas, on the other, as can be observed in children. In the first instance indeed, far from erasing unpleasure and replacing it with "wish fulfillment," the dreams of severely traumatized patients per-sistently and with great precision repeat the unpleasant trauma itself. The second instance is seen in the observation, by now well-known, of the "reel game," described by Freud in full detail when discussing his grandson Ernst. This description has been widely and variously analyzed and discussed. The reader will note that Freud does not restrict himself to a single solution but instead suggests several.

Chapter 3. As the first two chapters seem to end with uncer-tainties, we are all the more struck by the final sentence of chapter 2, a segue to the next one. In this sentence Freud dramatically affirms his "purpose" for the text as a whole: namely, to search for evidence of "the operation of tendencies *beyond* the pleasure principle, that is, of tendencies more primitive than it and independent of it."

To frame his evidence, Freud invokes his long experience of analytic work to vouch for the universality of transference in treat-ment: that is to say, for the fact that patients prefer to repeat the repressed than remember it and thus can be seen as under the sway of the compulsion to repeat. What's more, this applies not merely to pleasurable experiences but to unpleasurable ones as well. Despite all the disappointments occasioned by the transference—a repeti-tion of infantile disappointments—it is undone with great difficulty. To these exhibits Freud adds the examples of "nonneurotic" people whose lives are marked by repetitive patterns, most often painful, for which the subject does not seem responsible and that Freud calls "the constraint of destiny," using an episode from Tasso as a gripping poetic illustration.

Briefly recapitulating the examples given here and in chapter 2, the end of chapter 3 conveys the impression that for Freud the hypothesized compulsion to repeat consists of a kind of inexorable yet enigmatic theoretical residue that one must try to account for.

Chapter 4. The reader may approach chapters 4 and 5 jointly; both are prefaced by Freud's warning: "What follows is speculation…" In truth, it is not so easy to know what the author means by this term: probably substantial arguments that, admittedly, are not apodictic but that he holds dear, even though readers remain free to grapple with them according to their personal views. In fact, what will be at stake is none other than the theme of death, which, it is timely to recall, was a powerful presence for Freud in those years of war and mourning.

Moreover, when he admits that his speculation "often goes way back,"[1] he probably has in mind his earliest metapsychological texts (*Project for a Scientific Psychology, Studies on Hysteria*, etc.) and his privileged interlocutors at that time (Breuer, Fliess), now passed away.

Freud's speculative construction takes as its point of departure the beginnings of life on earth: "an undifferentiated vesicle of a substance that is susceptible to stimulation," immersed in an inanimate world that, moreover, is run through by quantities of energy incomparably greater than the energy within the vesicle. He indicates that he is returning, in a different mode, to the famous schematic picture of the psychic apparatus "included in the speculative section of … *Interpretation of Dreams*." The reader will see how Freud reconstructs this apparatus at once historically, mechanically, and genetically. Alongside the conscious and mnemic systems, the new element is the

---

1 Translator's note: the German phrase *oft weitausholende* is translated as "often far-fetched" by Strachey in the *Standard Edition*), making the reference to earlier texts obscure.

protective shield of the mental[2] system, an element that forms a sort of wall around this system. This shield is called the "stimulus barrier"; it maintains a boundary between internal and external levels of energy.

After describing pain and trauma as, respectively, limited or extended breaches in the stimulus barrier, leading to flooding of the vesicle by quantities of disorganizing unbound energy, Freud returns to the examples of trauma he has introduced in earlier chapters, endowing repetition with a more comprehensive metapsychological explanation. At stake is the binding of unbound energies flowing toward the breach, so that they can be evacuated according to the pleasure principle. As one will notice, Freud makes an important amendment to his theory of dreams: the presupposition of a preceding stage of binding, prior to the possibility of any wish fulfillment in line with the pleasure principle.

Chapter 5. But this broadening of the realm of the repetition compulsion entails relations with the drive-related sphere, which is to say essentially the excitations coming from within the organism. The drives (defined in rather different terms in earlier texts) are incorporated here into a general compulsion of a conservative nature, imposing "the restoration of an earlier state of things" as the sole aim of organic life. Given that "inanimate things existed before living ones", one can rightfully state that "the aim of all life is death." It is therefore in this very chapter that the notion of the "death drive" is introduced. A careful reader will be struck by Freud's spirited rheto-

---

2 Translator's note: In the French original, Laplanche uses the adjective *animique* to translate the German *seelisch*, pointing to a current debate among francophone psychoanalysts over the translation of *seelisch* and **psychisch**—a debate that to my knowledge has not been engaged in the Anglophone world until very recently. On the subject, see the entry on *Âme* (Soul) in *Traduire Freud* (Paris: PUF, 1989, pp. 77–78). In the context of this debate, I have suggested the term soulical to translate *seelisch* in order to retain the reference to the soul, as opposed to "psychic" (*psychisch*). The adjective "soulish" is another option, but I found that "soulical" established a clearer parallel between "psyche/psychic" and "soul/soulical". Following editorial guidelines, I have opted here for the English adjective "mental" in keeping with Strachey's translation in the *Standard Edition*.

ric, by his deliberately tautological argumentation: "It would be in contradiction to the conservative nature of the drives if the goal of life were a state of things which had never yet been attained."

Also worth noting are all the footnotes and additions that convey "repentances," nuances, and even, in a few lines at the end of the chapter, the entry onto the stage of the character Eros, who brings a substantial counterargument to the whole preceding development.

Chapter 6. Once the great dualism of life and death drives has been conceded, or rather posited, Freud resumes his speculative mode of reasoning with even more force in chapter 6, justifying himself with the fact that "people are seldom impartial where ultimate things . . . are concerned".

Though they give the impression of having been written somewhat off the cuff and though they tackle matters in haphazard fashion, these pages return to various questions left unresolved. First, authors who took an interest in the ultimate aims of life are given due credit: Fliess for his theory of feminine and masculine numbers, August Weismann for the well-argued differentiation between the mortal body (soma) and the immortal germinal plasma, Jung for his return to a drive-related monism, etc. But after dispensing with ideas deemed incompatible with his own, Freud finds himself contending with the major overhaul of his theory of the drives, an overhaul that does not replace the components of the former theory term by term but links them together in a rather different way. The life drives or sexual drives in particular raise specific problems: it must first be noted that, like the death drives, they are guided by the repetition compulsion. But what do they repeat? Freud here ventures to shift directly from reality to myth, invoking Aristophanes' theory of the origins of love in Plato's Symposium: the myth originates in double human beings that Zeus then chopped into two halves, each desperately striving to reconnect with its other half. It is clear, in any case, that the repetition compulsion is not exclusively bound to the death drives.

I will leave it to readers to go over, with pen in hand, those passages in chapter 6 where Freud raises new ideas: the experiments on the duration of life, sadism and masochism, etc.

Chapter 7. A mere two and a half pages long (not including an extended footnote that spans half a page), chapter 7 strives to be conclusive but cannot avoid raising a myriad of new questions. This chapter, once again centering on the pleasure principle, examines its relations with various concepts highlighted throughout the text: repetition, the life and death drives, bound and unbound processes, etc. For good measure, new conceptual tools such as "tendency" and "function" are introduced with a view to better analyzing the "pleasure principle." Let us retain a few key phrases punctuating a development that "raises a host of other questions to which we can at present find no answer":

> The binding of a [drive-related] impulse would be a pre-liminary function designed to prepare the excitation for its final elimination in the pleasure of discharge.

> The pleasure principle seems actually to serve the death drives.

> [T]he life drives . . . emerg[e] as breakers of the peace and constantly produc[e] tensions whose release is felt as pleasure—while the death drives seem to do their work unobtrusively.

Conclusion

Among the major concepts in this text that raise questions for Freud's psychoanalytic and philosophical posterity, I will foreground four: repetition, the binding-unbinding pair, the death drive, and reliance on speculation.

The notion of repetition was well received from the outset in psychoanalytic circles, given that its clinical references, as Freud recalled them himself, are frequent and evident; it applies to traumatic situations of all sorts, extreme or minor, collective or individual. Such situations are repeated in a variety of ways: in real life, in dreams, in the transference. An article by Edward Bibring published in 1943 (*Psa. Quart.* XII, pp. 436–519) differentiated two aspects of the notion: a *repetitive* tendency dependent on the id and a *restitutive* tendency that aims to restore the pretraumatic state and is ascribable to the ego. These two orientations lead us to stress that although repetition is no doubt an inert consequence of trauma it also belongs to the therapeutic armamentarium—whether spontaneous or deliberate—used in dealing with trauma. In this sense, repetition contributes to the binding attempts of the psychic apparatus in the face of traumatizing energy inflows.

We see how the notion of repetition leads to the notions of *binding* and *unbinding*. The opposition between free and bound energies dates back to Freud's community of thought with Breuer in *Studies on Hysteria*. Even though the two authors noticeably differ in how each uses the notions, in Freud's work, including the present text, we find them joined both with the notions of unconscious and primary process and, on the other hand, with the notions of preconscious and secondary process. The question that pervades the entire text is knowing how psychic energy can and must be bound in order to be capable of discharge. The main answer is provided by Freud's description and analysis of the "reel game" in chapter 2. This game can be seen as a model of the process of symbolization or symbolizing substitution, even though Freud does not use these terms. The substitution occurs following two stages and between three pairs of terms: first the mother, absent or present, is replaced with the reel, which is sent away and then brought back by the child's action; second, the reel, absent or present, is replaced with a simple pair of phonemes (o-o-o . . . da-a-a). This model thus replaces a pair of objects, then a pair of signs, with a pair of signifiers, having

125

meaning only through their contiguity and opposition.

One might wonder whether terms like symbolization, working through, trauma, and traumatic neurosis are inscribed in an attempted conceptualization that would draw metapsychology in the direction of a theory of trauma in which psychic conflict would be mainly between forces of binding and forces of unbinding. It is in this sense, among others, that we can understand the introduction of the death drive; for this purpose, structural aspects of the evolution of Freud's thought must be brought to bear: with the introduction of narcissism, a unified and all-encompassing theory seems to open up, a theory that under the name Eros joins sexuality in a drive-related whole that aims to bind energies and form ever larger and more unified objects. Freud himself noted that at this stage in his reflection he had apparently drawn closer to Jung's monistic views. This Eros, equally narcissistic and object-related, conceals the persistent presence of self-preservative biological mechanisms, even while delegating the sexual to them [*tout en les vicariant*]; but, even worse, it no longer takes account of the destructive and desta-bilizing aspects of the sexual *in itself*. This proposition, which Freud will stand by right to the end—that in the essence of sexuality there is something contrary and hostile to the ego—can no longer be heard, as soon as the psychoanalytic sexual finds itself reduced to the eternal paean of universal love, which, precisely, is in keeping with the ego.

Before the ominous danger of a victory of some hegemonic narcissistic Eros, an imperious need arises—in real life and in the pro-gression of Freud's thought alike—to reaffirm the drive in its most radical form: in its "daemonic" form, strictly obeying primary pro-cess and the compulsion of fantasy.[3] From this perspective (which is

---

3 Translator's note: It is to be noted that Laplanche uses the French word *fantaisie* rather than *fantasme* to render the German *Phantasie* (the French phrase is la *con-trainte de la fantaisie*). He thus follows Daniel Lagache's recommendation to prefer *fantaisie* over *fantasme* in order to convey at once the fantasying activity (*Phantasieren*) and the result of the activity itself, both of which are included in the English *fantasy*, according to Laplanche (see the entry on *Fantaisie* in **Traduire Freud**, pp. 104–106).

my perspective), the so-called death drive would consist in nothing but the reinstatement of the untamed pole of sexuality, and the ruling polarity would involve *sexual death drives* and *sexual life drives*. I use these terms cautiously, bearing in mind that the words "life" and "death" refer primarily not to biological life and death but to their "analogues" in the life of the soul and in psychic conflict and that the kind of death that is pointed to is, first and foremost, the death of the individual, not the death of the other: the death drive cannot be reduced to an "aggressive drive" directed outward.

The resort to speculation, which opens chapter 4, itself deserves extensive development not limited to the present text: for example, chapter 7 of *The Interpretation of Dreams* is seen by Freud as "speculative," and the same qualifier may be applied to entire sections of *Totem and Taboo, Moses and Monotheism,* and other works.

Speculation is defined here as "an attempt to follow out an idea consistently, out of curiosity to see where it will lead." The starting idea is the idea of the "vesicle" of "living substance," as we saw at the beginning of chapter 4, a vesicle that is constantly subject to the danger of a return to the level of the inanimate substance that surrounds it. In my view, the "curiosity" to see where it will lead is aligned with another characteristic of this text: the freedom in Freud's style and conceptual choices (in a whole section of the text, in chapter 5, his exposition tackles life drives as if they were negligible entities, suggested by all the tiny addenda), as well as in relation to possible arguments from other authors, which he sometimes sweeps away in passing in the course of developing his thought.

On the topic of speculation, I would like to conclude by pointing out the parallel that arises with Karl Popper and his model of "conjecture." Like Freud, Popper proposes a rather strict speculative logic that starts with the conceded postulates of a theory complemented by proven facts; imagination does not lose its rights, but it remains guided by the rationality of the argumentation. However, the aim of the process is a very different one for each thinker: for Popper, the point is to seek and encounter contradiction (falsification by experiment, refutation by reasoning), which would force a change in the model (or parts of it)[4]; for Freud, even though he declares himself "ready . . . to abandon a path that we have followed for a time, if it seems to be leading to no good end," it is clear that he is not interested in debate and feels that it is "perfectly legitimate to reject remorselessly theories which are contradicted by the very first steps in the analysis of observed facts." On this subject, the pages dealing with critical reflection at the end of chapter 6 are worth a read.

Finally, and short of being comprehensive, let us recall the dates of the three texts that punctuate the period when the notion of the "death drive" is being formulated: 1920; 1926; 1930. In the present text, Freud claims that he is giving himself over, as if passively, to scientific curiosity; in 1926, in "Inhibitions, Symptoms and Anxiety," a text that revisits neurotic conflict as a whole, no dynamic role is assigned the opposition between life drives and death drives; in 1930, in *Civilization and Its Discontents*, Freud writes: "To begin with it was only tentatively that I put forward the views I have developed here, but in the course of time they have gained such a hold upon me that I can no longer think in any other way." A cycle of Freudian speculation would thus come to a close, between the two terms of *curiosity* and *hold*, a cycle likely to open up to other terms, including a more primal term: *exigency*.

Translated from the French by Dorothée Bonnigal-Katz

4See my article: "Levels of Proof" in *Sexual*, PUF, 2007 (*Freud and the Sexual*, Unconscious in Translation, 2011).

BIBLIOGRAPHY
OF WORKS BY JEAN LAPLANCHE

The following is incomplete is several respects. A complete list of Laplanche's writings, collected and uncollected, of all translations of his work and of all video and audio recordings is being prepared and will be available on the web site of the Fondation Laplanche.

1960   *L'Inconscient : une étude psychanalytique* in collaboration with Serge Leclaire.
>   Presented at the VI Colloque de Bonneval. Proceedings of the Colloque *L'Inconscient* were published by Desclée de Brouwer, Paris, 1966 in a volume containing other interventions by Laplanche.
>
>   Republished in *Problématiques IV. L'inconscient et le ça.* Paris: P.U.F., 1981.

>   E: *The Unconscious: A Psychoanalytic Study* Trans. Patrick Coleman. *Yale French Studies*, no. 48, 1972.

1961   *Hölderlin et la question du père.* Paris: P.U.F., 1961.

>   E: *Hölderlin and the Question of the Father.* Ed. and trans. Luke Carson. Introduction by Rainer Nägele. Victoria, BC: ELS Editions, 2007.

1964   *Fantasme originaire, fantasmes des origines, origines du fantasme* in collaboration with J.-B. Pontalis. Les Temps Modernes, #215, Volume 19, April 1964.

>   1985 Republished in the series *Textes du XXe siècle* with a new introduction by the authors. Paris: Hachette, 1985.

>   E: *Primal Fantasy, Fantasies of Origins, Origins of Fantasy,* Ed. and trans. Jonathan House in this volume. *Laplanche*, Dominique Scarfone, New York: Unconscious in Translation, 2015.

>   *Fantasy and the Origins of Sexuality;* International Journal of Psychoanalysis, vol. 49, 1968. [Reprinted in *Formations of Fantasy,* ed. Victor Burgin et al, Methuen, 1986; also reprinted in *Unconscious Phantasy,* ed. Ricardo Steiner, London: Karnac Books, 2003].

1967   *Vocabulaire de la psychanalyse* in collaboration with J.-B. Pontalis. Paris: P.U.F.

E: *The Language of Psycho-Analysis*. Trans. D. Nicholson-Smith. New York: Norton, 1973.

1970   *Vie et mort en psychanalyse*. Paris: Flammarion, 1970.

2nd edition 1971, includes *Dérivation des entités psychanalytiques*

E: *Life and Death in Psychoanalysis*. Trans. J. Mehlman. Baltimore: Johns Hopkins University Press, 1976. Includes *Derivation of Psychoanalytic Entities*

1970-73   Lectures given at the *Sorbonne-Université de Paris VII*, for his course within the UER des Sciences Humaines, published in the journal *Psychanalyse à l'université*; and then in **Problématiques I. L'angoisse**. Paris: P.U.F., 1980.
1970-1971 : L' « Angst » dans la névrose
1971-1972 : L'angoisse dans la topique
1972-1973 : L'angoisse morale

1973-75   Lectures given at the *Sorbonne-Université de Paris VII*, for his course within the UER des Sciences Humaines, published in the journal *Psychanalyse à l'université*; and then in **Problématiques II. Castration. Symbolisations**. Paris: P.U.F., 1980.
1973-1974 : La castration, ses précurseurs et son destin
1974-1975 : Symbolisations

E: Extract: Lecture 20 May, 1975. Trans. Arthur Goldhammer. *Literary Debate : Texts and Contexts*, Ed. Dennis Hollier and Jeffrey Mehlman. New York: The New Press, 1999.

1975-77   Lectures given at the *Sorbonne-Université de Paris VII*, for his course within the UER des Sciences Humaines, published in the journal *Psychanalyse à l'université*; and then in **Problématiques III. La sublimation**. Paris: P.U.F., 1980.
1975-1976 : Pour situer la sublimation
1976-1977 : Faire dériver la sublimation

E: Extract: **To Situate Sublimation**. Trans. Richard Miller. *October*, No. 28, Spring, 1984.

1977-79   Lectures given at the *Sorbonne-Université de Paris VII*, for his course within the UER des Sciences Humaines, published in the journal *Psychanalyse à l'université*; and then in **Problématiques IV. L'Inconsient et le Ça**. Paris: P.U.F., 1981.
1977-1978 : La référence à l'inconscient
1978-1979 : Problématique du ça

E: *The Unconscious and the Id*, Trans. Luke Thurston with Lindsay Watson, London: Rebus Press, 1999.

1979-84   Lectures given at the *Sorbonne-Université de Paris VII*, for his course within the UER des Sciences Humaines, published in the journal *Psychanalyse à l'université*; and then in **Problématiques V. Le baquet – Transcendance du transfert**. Paris: P.U.F., 1987.
          1979-1980 : Le psychanalyste et son baquet
          1980-1981 : Le descriptif et le prescriptif
          1983-1984 : La transcendance du transfer

1987   *Nouveaux fondements pour 1a psychanalyse*. Paris: P.U.F., 1987.

          E: *New Foundations for Psychoanalysi*s, trans. David Macey, Oxford: Basil Blackwell, 1989.

                 New Foundations for Psychoanalysis, trans. Robert Stein, New York: Unconscious in Translation, forthcoming.

1989   *Traduire Freud*. In collaboration with A. Bourguignon, P. Cotet, F. Roberts. Paris: P.U.F., 1989.

          E: Extract: **Translating Freud**, trans. Maev de la Guardia and Bertrand Vichyn, in Translating Freud, ed. Darius Gray Ornston, New Haven: Yale University Press, 1992.

1989-90   Lectures given at the *Sorbonne-Université de Paris VII*, for his course within the UER des Sciences Humaines, published in the journal *Psychanalyse à l'université*; and then in **Problématiques VI. L'après-coup**. Paris: P.U.F., 2006.
          1989-1990 : La « Nachträglichkeit » dans l'après-coup

1991-92   Lectures given at the *Sorbonne-Université de Paris VII*, for his course within the UER des Sciences Humaines, published in the journal *Psychanalyse à l'université*; and then in **Problématiques VII : Le fourvoiement biologisant de la sexualité chez Freud suivi de Biologisme et biologie**. Paris: P.U.F., initially published in 1993 by Synthélabo .

          E: **The Temptation of Biology: Freud's Theories of Sexuality**. Trans. Donald Nicholson-Smith. New York: Unconscious in Translation, 2015.

          E: Extract: **Exigency and Going-Astray**. Trans. Vincent Ladmiral and Nicholas Ray. *Psychoanalysis, Culture and Society*, 11, 2006, pp. 164-189.

1992   *La révolution copernicienne inachevée (Travaux 1967-1992).* Paris: Aubier, 1992.

E: English translations of works contained in this volume

1968   **Interpreting [with] Freud** *(Interpréter [avec] Freud).* Trans. Vincent Ladmiral and Nicholas Ray, *Psychoanalysis, Culture and Society.* vol. 11, 2006.

1979   **A Metapsychology put to the Test of Anxiety** *(Une métapsychologie à lépreuve de l'angoisse). International Journal of Psychoanalysis,* vol. 62, 1981.

1984   **The Drive and its Object-source: its fate in the transference** *(La pulsion et son objet-source. Son destin dans le transfer).*

Trans. Martin Stanton *Jean Laplanche: Seduction, Translation and the Drives,* ed. John Fletcher and Martin Stanton, London: Institute of Contemporary Arts, 1992.

Trans. Leslie Hill. *Essays on Otherness,* ed. John Fletcher, London: Routledge, 1999.

1987   **Specificity of Terminological Problems in the Translation of Freud** *(Spécificité des problèmes terminologiques dans la traduction de Freud). International Review of Psychoanalysis,* vol. 18, 1991.

1988   **The Wall and the Arcade** *(Le mur et l'arcade).* Trans. Martin Stanton. Op. cit.

1989   **Psycholanalysis, Time and Translation** *(Temporalité et traduction. Pour une remise au travail de la philosophie du temps).* Trans. Martin Stanton. Op. cit.

1990   **Implantation, Intromission** *(Implation, intromission).* Trans Luke Thurston, *Essays on Otherness,* ed. John Fletcher, London: Routledge, 1999.

1990   **Time and the Other** *(Le temps et l'autre).* Trans. Luke Thurston. *Essays on Otherness,* ed. John Fletcher, London: Routledge, 1999.

1991 **Interpretation Between Determinism and Hermeneutics: A Restatement of the Problem** *(L'interprétation entre déterminisme et herméneutique: une nouvelle position de la question)* Trans. Philip Slotkin. Essays on Otherness, ed. John Fletcher, London: Routledge, 1999.

1992 **Masochism and the General Theory of Seduction** *(Masochisme et théorie de la séduction généralisée)*. Trans. Luke Thurston. *Essays on Otherness*, ed. John Fletcher, London: Routledge, 1999.

1992 **Transference: its Provocation by the Analyst** *(Du transfert : sa provocation par l'analyste)*. Trans. Luke Thurston. *Essays on Otherness*, ed. John Fletcher, London: Routledge, 1999.

1992 **The Unfinished Copernican Revolution** *(La révolution copernicienne inachevée)*. Trans. Luke Thurston *Essays on Otherness*, ed. John Fletcher, London: Routledge, 1999.

1997 *"The Theory of Seduction and the Problem of the Other."* Trans. Luke Thurston. *International Journal of Psychoanalysis*, vol. 78, no. 4, 1997.

1998 *"From the Restricted to the Generalized Theory of Seduction."* In *Seduction, Suggestion, Psychoanalysis*. Ed. Jose Corveleyn and Philippe Van Haute. Leuven University Press and Duquesne University Press, 1998.

1999 *Entre séduction et inspiration : L'Homme.* Paris: P.U.F., 1999.

E: **Between Seduction and Inspiration**. Trans. Jeffrey Mehlman, New York: Unconscious in Translation, forthcoming 2015

E: Other English translations of works contained in this volume

1992 **Notes on Afterwardsness**. Trans. Martin Stanton *Jean Laplanche: Seduction, Translation and the Drives*, ed. John Fletcher and Martin Stanton, London: Institute of Contemporary Arts, 1992. Taken from a recorded conversation with Martin Stanton. Later augmented by Laplanche and published with the same title in *Essays on Otherness*, ed. John Fletcher, London: Routledge, 1999. Also, in a French version in *Entre séduction et inspiration : l'homme*. Paris, PUF 1999

1992 **The Unfinished Copernican Revolution** *(La révolution copernicienne inachevée)*.

1992 **Seduction, Persecution, Revelation** *(Séduction, persécution, révélation)*. Trans. Philip Slotkin. *The International Journal of Psychoanalysis*, vol. 76, no. 4, 1996

1994 **Psychoanalysis as Anti-hermeneutics** *(La psychanalyse comme anti-herméneutique)*. Trans. Luke Thurston. *Radical Philosophy*, no. 79, Sept./Oct., 1996.

1995 **The So-Called 'Death-Drive': a Sexual Drive** (La soi-disant pulsion de mort : une pulsion sexuelle). Trans. Luke Thurston. *The Death-Drive*. Ed. Rob Weatherill, London: Rebus Press, 1999. Reprinted in *The British Journal of Psychotherapy*, vol. 20, no. 4, 2004.

1996 **Aims of the Psychoanalytic Process** *(Buts du processus psychanalytique)*. *Journal of European Psychoanalysis*, no. 5, Spring/Fall, 1997.

1996 **Psychoanalysis: Myths and Theories** (La psychanalyse: mythes et théorie.) Trans. *Psychoanalytic Quarterly*, vol. 77, no. 3, 2003.

1998 **Narrativity and Hermeneutics: some propositions** *(Narrativité et herméneutique: quelque propositions.)* Trans. John Fletcher. *New Formations*, no. 48, Winter, 2002/3

1999 **Sublimation and/or Inspiration** (Sublimation et/ou inspiration.) Trans. John Fletcher. *New Formations*, no. 48, Winter, 2002-3.

2007 *Sexual : La sexualité élargie au sens freudien 2000-2006*. Paris: P.U.F.

E: *Freud and the Sexual: Essays 2000-2006*, ed. John Fletcher; trans. John Fletcher, Jonathan House, Nicholas Ray. New York: Unconscious in Translation, (IPB) 2011

E: Other English translations of works contained in this volume

2000 **Sexuality and Attachment in Metapsychology** *(Sexualité et l'attachement dans la metapsychologie.)* Trans. Susan Fairfield. *Infantile Sexuality and Attachment*. Ed. Daniel Widlöcher. New York: Other Press, 2002.

2000 **Closing and Opening of the Dream: Must Chapter VII be Rewritten?** *(Rêve et communication : faut-il réécrire me chapitre VII?)* Trans. Mira Reinberg and Thomas Pepper. *Dreams of Interpretation: A Century down the Royal Road.* Ed. Catherin Liu et al. Minneapolis: University of Minnesota Press, 2007.

2003 **Gender, Sex, and the Sexual** *(Le genre, le sexe, le sexual.)"* Trans.Susan Fairfield. *Gender and Sexuality*, vol. 8, no. 2, 2007.

Index

aberrations, sexual, 15; *see also* perversion
abuse, sexual, 22-23
accidental, 16, 52, 56, 88, 98, 120; *see also*
    contingent
adaptation, 15, 20, 38, 45, 57, 60, 75
address to, 44, 54, 114
adult-child relation, 22, 26-27, 49-54, 56,
    58, 61, 80-82, 85-87, 111
afterwardsness, xii, 25, 92; *see*
    après-coup
agency
    ego-as-agency, 30
aggression, 56, 76
aim
    of analytic work, 35, 38, 75
    of drive & of instinct, 15, 28, 107-
    110, 112-113, 122-123, 125-126
âme, xi, 122; *see also* soul
American, 14, 23-24, 30, 36, 40
American Psychoanalytic Association, 6
anaclisis, x, xii, 11, 72; *see* leaning-on
André, Jacques, 5, 33
anglophone, xii, 122
animique, xi, 122; *see also âme*
anlehnung, x, xii, 11, 72; *see also*
    leaning-on
Anna O, 24, 74
anobjectal, 17-18, 49
anthropology, viii, 44, 66, 97
anxiety, 39, 64, 83, 128
apparatus, psychic; apparatus of the
    soul, , xii, 14, 45, 51, 55, 57, 95, 119,
    121, 125; *see also* soul
applied, 37; *see also* extramural
après-coup, xii, 25-27, 48, 51, 59, 92-94,
    105; *see also* afterwardsness;
    Nachträglichkeit
archaeology, 4, 46, 73
Aristarchus, 4
Aristophanes, 123
Aristotle, 82
arousal, 82, 86, 98, 100, 114
asymmetry, 53, 56
aufhebung, 27
autoerotism, 16-18, 20, 32, 73, 81, 93,

109-114; *see also* drive
autohypnosis, 74

Bachelard, Gaston, 31
Balint, Michael, 17
baquet, 35, 45, 60; *see* tub
bedrock, 95
Befriedigung, 110
beginning, 17-18, 27, 58, 72, 78, 91,
    99-100, 107, 111-112, 121, 127
Bibring, Grete, 125
binding, 30-31, 34, 106, 122, 124-126; *see*
    also unbinding
biological, viii, 10, 15, 19-20, 29, 33, 35,
    42-46, 49, 51, 84, 86, 88-90, 100, 107,
    109, 119, 126-127
birth, 35, 46, 83, 86, 100, 109, 113
bisexuality, 102, 105
Bonaparte, Marie, 80
Bonneval, 12-14, 58
borderline, 62
Bourguignon, André, 5
breast, 16, 18, 58, 74, 108, 110-112
Breuer, Josef, 41, 74, 121, 125
Brücke, Ernst Wilhelm von, 43

Calvino, Italo, viii
candidates, at analytic institutes, 38
castration, 35, 39-40, 43, 95-96, 99-100
catharsis, 41-42, 74
cathexis, 103, 110
censorship, 105
centered, vii, 8, 22, 38, 56, 64-67, 124; *see*
    also decentered
childhood, 22, 78, 81, 83, 85, 96, 109
communication, 43, 55, 104
compromised message, 21, 54, 57-58; *see*
    also enigma
compulsion, 33, 120-123, 126; *see also*
    exigency; Zwang
contiguity, 15-16, 30, 58, 126
contingent, 16, 27, 50, 52, 56, 75, 97; *see*
    also accidental
Copernicus, xi, 3-4, 8, 12, 34, 38, 63-66,
    79, 94

137

Cotet, Piere, 5
creux, 61; *see* hollowedout

Darwin, Charles, 3, 64
daydream, 74-75, 90, 101-104, 106
death, 5, 121-122
decentered, 8, 52-53, 65-66; *see also*
  centered
deferred action, 25, 92; *see après-coup*
derivation, 15-16, 22, 30, 57
desexualized, 48
desire
  hallucinatory satisfaction of, 32
  to become an analyst, 38
determinism, 46
deviant, 15-16, 22, 49-50; *see also*
  perversion
displacement, 13, 17-18, 103
drive
  aggressive drive, 76, 107-108, 127
  death drive, 15, 32-34, 122-128
  life drive, 32-34
  use of term versus instinct, 15-19

école, 36, 72
ego, 8, 28-34, 38, 42, 44, 63-65, 76, 82,
  106, 108-109, 112, 125-126
Einstein, Albert, xiii, 50
Emma, 24-25, 51
enigma, 53-57, 60-62, 66, 72, 99, 121
erogenous zones, 113-114
Eros, 33-34, 123-126
erotogenic, 16, 26, 56, 114
étayage, xii, 11, 15, 72; *see also*
  leaning-on
étrangièrité, xiii; *see* strangerness
exigency, 7, 9, 33, 128; *see also* compulsion; Zwang
extramural, 37; *see also* applied

Fairbairn, Ronald, 17
falsification, 36, 40, 128
fantasy, ix-x, 9, 11, 16, 18-20, 22-23, 39,
  43, 46, 56, 69, 71-72, 74-80, 84-91,
  93-115, 126

father, 50, 52, 67, 83, 87, 89, 96-97, 100,
  106-107
Ferenczi, Sandor, 51, 53, 85-86
Fliess, Wilhelm, 51, 59, 80, 82-83, 86-87,
  92, 121, 123
foreclusion, 93-94
Foucault, Michel, 67

geocentrism, 8
gestalt, 8, 112

hallucination, 32, 47, 74, 93, 110
Hegel, G. W. F., 27
heliocentrism, 5, 66; *see also* geocentrism
helplessness, 83; *see also* Hilflösigkeit
hereditary, 87, 96-97
hermeneutics, 12, 46, 63-64
Hilflösigkeit, 49; *see also* helplessness
Hölderlin, Friedrich, 57, 67
hollowedout, 61; *see also* creux
homeostasis, 119
humanization, 27
Hyppolite, Jean, 30
hysteria, xiii, 22-24, 28, 50, 74, 81-84, 87,
  89, 101-102, 105, 121, 125

id, 30, 35, 43, 59, 65, 97, 109, 125
identification, 10, 19, 30, 44, 50, 55, 103
imagination, 23, 74-75, 77-80, 89-90,
  92-93, 96-97, 100-102, 105-107, 109,
  127; *see also* fantasy
implantation, 22, 27, 29, 57, 62-63; *see
  also* inscription
indeterminacy, 25, 27
inscription, 14, 24, 36, 41, 43-44, 46, 53,
  57, 105, 126; *see also* implantation
inspiration, 65, 73, 101
instincts, 16, 19-20, 29, 33, 49, 52, 75,
  107-108, 110, 113; *see also* drive
intersubjective, 27, 55
introjection, 74-76, 85-86
intromission, 62-63
investment, 29, 31-32, 103
ipsocentric, 8, 63, 65
Isaacs, Susan, 101, 107-108, 110

Dominique Scarfone MD (*author*) is full professor at the Department of Psychology and Psychiatry of the *Université de Montréal* where he teaches psychoanalytic theory, does clinical supervision, and conducts research. A psychoanalyst in private practice, he is a member of the *Société* and of the *Institut psychanalytique de Montréal*, as well as the *Canadian Psychoanalytic Society and Institute*. He was associate editor of the *International Journal of Psychoanalysis* and served on the boards of the *Canadian Journal of Psychoanalysis* and the *Revue Française de psychanalyse*. He has published four books: *Jean Laplanche, Oublier Freud? Mémoire pour la psychanalyse, Les Pulsions*, and *Quartiers aux rues sans nom*. He co-edited *Un-represented States and the Construction of Meaning*, with Howard Levine and Gail Reed. He lives in Montreal.

Dorothée Bonnigal-Katz (*translator*) is a psychoanalyst based in London and Leamington Spa (West Midlands, UK). A member of *The Site for Contemporary Psychoanalysis* and the *College of Psychoanalysts (UK)*, she is the founder and the clinical lead of the *Psychosis Therapy Project* at Islington Mind. She is a leading translator of psychoanalytic theory and philosophy. She has translated essays and books by Laurence Kahn, Jean Laplanche, Dominique Scarfone, Guy Rosolato, Pierre Legendre, Christopher Bollas and Miguel de Beistegui, among others.

Co-editors:

Jonathan House teaches courses on Freud and Laplanche in the Psychoanalytic Studies Program of Columbia University's Institute for Comparative Literature and Society. At Columbia he is also on the faculty of the Department of Psychiatry and of the Center for Psychoanalytic training and Research where he is a Training and Supervising Analyst. At Laplanche's invitation, he agreed to serve on the *Conseil Scientifique* of the *Fondation Laplanche*. In 2010 he founded a publishing house, The Unconscious in Translation, dedicated to translating and promoting the work of Jean Laplanche and other notable French psychoanalysts. He has been Secretary of the American Psychoanalytic Association and remains on its Board of Directors. He currently serves on the Free Association Work Group of the Committee on Conceptual Integration for the International Psychoanalytic Association. He practices psychiatry and psychoanalysis in New York City.

Julie Slotnick studied comparative literature at Columbia University and the Freie Universität Berlin. She works in New York as a freelance translator and editor.

Book design, Bill Schultz
Copy-editor, Michael Farrin